Do You See This Woman?

By
Aaron Kemple

Published by
Spiritbuilding Publishers
9700 Ferry Road, Waynesville, OH 45068

(800) 282–4901

DO YOU SEE THIS WOMAN?
By Aaron Kemple

ISBN: 978–1–955285–45–2

Printed in the USA by D & E Printing, Brownsburg, IN
dandeprinting.com

Spiritbuilding
PUBLISHERS

spiritbuilding.com
Spiritual equipment for the contest of life

Table of Contents

Introduction

Here is the focus of this book:

- To "see" various women in Scripture in a variety of situations.
- To put on heaven's glasses to view these women with God's eyes.
- To reshape how we see God, ourselves, and others.

In this book, you will see women who are in a variety of life circumstances. You will see married women and those who are divorced. You'll observe women who are rich, and in leadership positions, but you'll also look at a woman who only had two coins left. Jesus is asking, "Do you see this woman?"

In every chapter, you will be challenged to see these various women of the Bible from God's perspective. My hope is that through studying these ladies of Scripture that you will have a change in vision in 3 ways:

1. How you see God.
2. How you see yourself.
3. How you see others.

Let's start the journey to see with a fresh, renewed godly perspective.

Lesson 1
Vision Correction:
Turning on the Divine Spotlight

We may have great eyesight, but still have poor vision.

Everyone needs a new set of glasses.

In order to see the world properly, we cannot rely on our own human vision. Left to our own perspective, how we see others and how we see ourselves will only be distorted images. When the lenses through which we view all experiences and relationships are based upon man's wisdom, then we will always be out of focus. It's like when you stand in front of one of those carnival mirrors—the image is all out of whack.

When the elderly prophet Samuel was sent by God to anoint the next king, God had to correct Samuel's spiritual vision. God said:

> Do not look on his appearance or on the height of his stature, because I have rejected him. For the LORD sees not as man sees: man looks on the outward appearance, but the LORD looks on the heart. (1 Samuel 16:7)

Samuel saw David's oldest brother, Eliab, and assumed Eliab was going to be the next king. But Samuel was looking only at the surface level. He was looking at the outward shell of Eliab. On the outside, Eliab looked like a king. But God knew Eliab didn't have the right heart. God saw the inside of Eliab and rejected him as king. God doesn't see as man sees.

In Luke 7:44, Jesus asked the question, "Do you see this woman?" He asked this of a man who clearly needed a change of perspective. Simon the Pharisee was one of the Jewish religious leaders. He, like most of the Jewish leadership, was self-righteous and did not see his own need for God's saving grace (Luke 18:9). Since Simon didn't see himself properly in view of God's grace, it altered how he viewed others, including the sinful woman who was in his house to see Jesus.

We'll go in depth on the events of Luke 7:36–50 later, but for now let's appreciate that Jesus was constantly shining the divine spotlight on outcasts for the purpose of training others to see with His eyes. During His brief 3½ years of ministry, He called people to focus on those who were treated with contempt or dismissed. If you read through the gospel accounts, you will regularly find Jesus directing attention to people counted as worthless. He publicly highlighted these people to showcase their value and amazing character.

Sinners. Tax collectors. Harlots. Roman Centurions. Gentiles. Samaritans. Lepers.

And…women.

These groups were not valued at all by the Jewish leadership in those days. In fact, Jesus frequently pointed out that the Pharisees treated livestock better than they did these children of God (Luke 13:15–16; 14:5).

How Jesus looked at people is not how we as humans view others. Jesus is the Creator, and He never lost sight of the fact that He made man and woman in His own image (Genesis 1:26–27). He saw people as sons and daughters of God and children in need of salvation and compassion. As God who sees the heart, He saw amazing character in those who were judged by appearances.

But even His closest followers, the twelve apostles, needed constant vision correction by Jesus. The Twelve apostles were constantly trying to send people away. They "rebuked" those who brought kids to him (Mark 10:13) and they "rebuked" blind Bartimaeus for crying out to Jesus (Mark 10:48). They begged Jesus to send away the Gentile woman who was crying out to Him (Matthew 15:23).

Jesus responded in a way that continued to surprise His disciples. He wanted the kids by His side. He healed the blind man they tried to silence. He commended the great faith of the Gentile woman they wanted to send away. It was during times like these that the spiritual blindness of His disciples was exposed. The apostles needed to see with Jesus' eyes.

And that is what Jesus wants to do for all of us. He wants us to have new glasses. The way we see ourselves, God, and others needs to be remodeled to a heavenly vision.

Why does this matter for you and me?

Have you ever seen someone in one way, only to realize you were looking at that person from the completely wrong perspective? Once you were given more information and background, you saw that person in a new light?

Have you struggled with how you see yourself? Have you allowed how others see you and treat you affect how you see yourself? And when you see yourself in the wrong way, how does that affect your relationships with others?

Have you seen God as a God only of judgment and condemnation? Have you needed to reshape your vision of God to include grace, mercy, and compassion? If you have done that, how did it affect how you see yourself and others?

—Lesson 1 Discussion Questions—

1. Why is it so important for you to see yourself through God's eyes?

2. Have you allowed how others see you to affect how you see yourself?

3. Is it possible that you are struggling in your relationships because of how you "see" other people?

Lesson 2
Vision Correction:
Unhealthy Expectations

They tie up heavy burdens, hard to bear, and lay them on people's shoulders, but they are not willing to move them with their finger. (Matthew 23:4)

As MEN AND WOMEN OF GOD, we set expectations for ourselves and for others. Those expectations, however, must be realistic and biblical. Healthy expectations are set by properly understanding God's Word. Our expectations are shaped by our vision. How we see God, His Word, ourselves, and others, will determine the expectations we place on ourselves and others.

For starters—THE VIRTUOUS WIFE *or* the PERFECT UNATTAINABLE STANDARD?

Sometimes what happens in studying passages like the virtuous woman of Proverbs 31:10–31 is that we arrive at unhealthy conclusions and make unrealistic expectations. A passage like Proverbs 31, which is intended to be an encouragement to God's people (both male and female) can be used as a hammer to beat ourselves and others on the head with thoughts like, "You aren't measuring up."

When we dive into Scripture and do character studies, we must remember to have a balanced view. Let's set some things straight. Not one of those men and women of faith was flawless—all have sinned (Romans 3:23). Not one of the Bible "greats" always made every decision right. Not one of them always had it all together. We sometimes view our heroes in the Bible as "Super-Saints," and then we build up these unfair demands of ourselves and of others. We are trying to match ourselves and others up to some false picture we have concocted in our minds.

For example, those honestly seeking to please God may read about the Virtuous Woman of Proverbs 31 and turn her into Super-Perfect-Christian-Lady. Here's how it may play out in the believer's mind.

The "excellent wife" got all her chores done by 10:00 AM, had a multi-million dollar career in the clothing industry, and her kids were always well-behaved. She never lost her temper, she always cooked an extra casserole for the shut-ins, and she treated her husband with 100 percent respect and never neglected his "needs." She taught Bible classes better than they had ever been taught before, she had potlucks in her home regularly, and she always said just the right thing in the right way. This woman was a perfect specimen of health and beauty. She never ran out of steam, she never misspent any money, and she budgeted her time with complete efficiency and precision. This super wife woke up a half hour after she went to bed. *And*…she never complained…blah, blah, blah. If Mary Poppins was "practically perfect in every way," then this woman crushed Mary Poppins' record. Some of you may have burnt out your adrenal glands just reading this paragraph.

As well-meaning Christians study the Scripture, they may desperately spend all their efforts trying to live up to a standard that God never set for them. They keep falling short in their own estimation, and their other brethren "fail" as well. Those feelings can be sadly encouraged by leaders, teachers, parents, and demanding spouses that are looking down in disappointment because of their own internal issues and poor understanding of God's Word.

What happens then? You know, don't you? They (maybe even you) become drained, disabled, disillusioned, discouraged, and downright depressed. Haven't you at some point thrown up your hands thinking you can never get it all right? It's just painful sometimes, isn't it? You can never "get it all right" if your standard is unrealistic and unattainable. "Getting it right" should at least start with establishing what is "right."

Here are some additional points about the "excellent wife" of Proverbs 31—

She had help!

My wife, Anna, is very wise to point out that the woman of Proverbs 31 had "maidservants" (see v. 15)! So, a quick note to any husbands reading this, if you expect your wife to carry out all the jobs the Virtuous Woman did, then you'd better hire some help or help her out yourself!

She had a husband who trusted her, supported her, and praised her. His heart "safely trusted in her." She had a lot of freedom in their relationship to do her "thing." Look at all she did on her own while her husband was "at the gates." His words were words of affirmation and praise, and he led the kids in doing the same. This woman was given wings to fly, and she was able to flourish and grow even more because she is in a healthy relationship. She grew into these qualities.

Whatever we see here about this virtuous woman, we must remember that she developed these qualities over time. This passage is intended (I believe) to be a general, composite picture of the great qualities of a godly woman. It was never intended to be used as a ton of bricks to lay on a woman's shoulders. We are not to take this passage and expect that every godly woman excels at all of these things. The woman in Proverbs 31 grew into her skills and used them for her family and for God. She learned to be kind and wise. She's not flawless, she has grown mature in God.

Good news!

God receives you, just as you are, and He receives your fellow sisters and brothers also (Romans 15:7)! Those expectations that you dreamed up in your head most likely are not from God. They might be from misguided, yet well-intentioned teachers (or books) in your past, or it might come from others very close to you (like spouses or parents) who hold a standard that is impossible to meet. Even when we are not meeting God's expectations, remember that He is your loving Father, and His grace and mercy are with you every day as you grow in Him and walk with Jesus.

May God give us the spiritual vision correction to develop healthy expectations for ourselves and others.

—Lesson 2 Discussion—

1. How can the wrong expectations become a horrible burden that drives us to discouragement?

2. What must we remember about God's grace when it comes to expectations and our growth in Jesus Christ?

Lesson 3
Seeing a Woman Forgiven and Grateful

The Sinful Woman (Luke 7:36–50)

HAVE YOU NOTICED that Jesus was in a lot of people's homes for dinner? Jesus accepted invitations from all kinds of folks and went to their homes for a meal. He was an equal-opportunity dinner guest. He ate in the homes of the Jewish religious leaders (Luke 7:36; 11:37; 14:1), and He also shared a meal with the most despised sinners, the tax collectors (Luke 5:27–32). The "Son of Man has come eating and drinking," our Lord said of Himself (Luke 7:34).

Whether it was a Passover feast (John 13), or a meal with the Mary-Martha-Lazarus family (John 12), Jesus was constantly in homes sharing a few moments talking over dinner. Sometimes He even invited Himself to dinner, as in the case of Zacchaeus (Luke 19:1–6). On at least two occasions, Jesus was the host. He miraculously provided food for thousands of people, the 5,000 and the 4,000 (Matthew 14:21; 15:38).

These meals were filled with teachable moments. The hearts were revealed at dinner – critical hearts, proud hearts, unfaithful hearts and hearts full of incredible faith. Martha was upset that Mary wasn't helping serve, and Jesus gave her a lesson on priorities by pointing to Mary (Luke 10:38–42). The disciples (namely Judas) sharply criticized Mary during dinner for wasting expensive fragrant oil on Jesus, but the Lord held Mary up as an example for the whole world to see (Matthew 26; Mark 14; John 12). The 5,000 were fed to demonstrate that Jesus is the Bread of Life (John 6). On the night before Jesus was crucified, His disciples learned after supper about humility as He washed their feet (John 13).

The Jewish religious leaders were notorious for criticizing Jesus at these meals. They "watched him carefully" (Luke 14:1), because they were just waiting to pounce on Him for making a mistake (Luke 11:53–54). They were repulsed that Jesus didn't first wash His hands before dinner (Luke 11:37–38), and they grumbled against Him for receiving sinners and eating with them (Luke 15:2). It really upset them when He ate with tax collectors, because Jews who worked for the Roman government collecting taxes were considered the lowest sort of humans to many Jews (Luke 5:27–32; 19:7).

Jesus' divine character was on display at these meals. When in the home of Zacchaeus the tax collector, he said, "The Son of Man has come to seek and to save that which was lost" (Luke 19:10). This verse is considered by many as the theme for the book of Luke. The reason Jesus went to meals with people is because He wanted to save them. Whether it was a harlot who knew she was a sinner, or whether it was an expert in Moses' law who was self-righteous, Jesus ate with them. His offer of salvation was open for anyone.

This brings us to Luke 7, where Luke records a scandalous anointing of Jesus by a sinful woman. Where did this happen? In the house of a Jewish religious leader, Simon the Pharisee. Simon had invited Jesus over for dinner, along with other guests (Luke 7:36, 49).

Luke described this woman simply as, "a woman of the city, who was a sinner." What is her name? We don't know. What is her sin? We don't know. The conclusion many have made is that her sin was of a sexual nature. That seems like a very sound conclusion, but we don't know. Simon's inner thoughts tell us a little more when he considered "who and what sort of woman she was, for she is a sinner" (Luke 7:39). It makes me think that she was a woman of the night, a prostitute, by the way he described the woman. But again, we don't know for sure. What we do know is that her sins were many, according to Jesus (Luke 7:47). And we know that whoever she was and whatever she had done, Simon was disgusted.

An embarrassing display by a despicable woman, or a precious demonstration of a broken heart touched by grace—which is it?

There was some kind of "Jesus Broadcast Network" in Palestine during those days, because reports and news spread everywhere Jesus went. It was widely publicized when Jesus came into a city, or even to a specific home.

It is my conclusion that the woman had some previous encounter with Jesus, and He had forgiven her of her sins. She now comes in to demonstrate her love and gratitude for His mercy. Jesus' explanation of her act of anointing shows that her anointing of Jesus was out of love and gratitude for having been forgiven of her sins. She loved much, which means she had been forgiven of much. So, it seems to me that she had at least one previous encounter with Jesus where she had heard His preaching and had come to Him for forgiveness. This overwhelming spirit of thankfulness led her to enter a Pharisee's house and endure scowls and condemnation in order to pour out her love upon Jesus.

She is behind him at his feet.

The humility of this sinful woman is clear. She does not come to His face. She does not stand in front of Him. Her positioning indicated how she saw Jesus and her place before him. This makes me think of Abigail who was called by David to be his wife, a wife of the future king. Even with the prospects of being Queen, Abigail viewed herself as a "servant to wash the feet of David's servants" (1 Samuel 25:41). That is the heart of this woman, she is behind Jesus at His feet, washing His feet with her tears. The forgiveness granted to her by Jesus did not lift her up with pride, rather it brought her to her knees. It also reminds me of Ezra as he is overwhelmed by his sins and the sins of the people. He could not so much as lift his face to God, and he was brought to his knees (Ezra 9:5–6).

This mindset is contrasted throughout the book of Luke. Those whose hearts were proud, unthankful, stubborn, and self-righteous are exposed by Jesus as He shined heaven's light on them. That same light also displayed to the whole world the amazing heart of the outcasts: the lepers, Samaritans, harlots, tax collectors, Gentiles, Roman officers, and the women.

Here are several examples:

- The tax collectors who were baptized by John the Baptist while the Pharisees rejected God's will and John's baptism (Luke 7).
- The good Samaritan versus the Levite and Priest (Luke 10).
- The older brother and the younger brother (Prodigal son, Luke 15).

- The Rich man and Lazarus (Luke 16).
- The two men who went to the temple to pray (Luke 18).
- Pharisees who devoured widow's houses and the widow who gave her last two coins to God (Luke 20—21).
- The rulers mocking Jesus while He was on the cross, and the thief who begged Him for mercy (Luke 23).

Simon had self-righteous condemnation while looking at Jesus' face. This woman poured out her soul from behind the Lord at his feet to express how thankful she was for Jesus' mercy upon her.

She anointed Jesus—use all your senses here.

Take time to picture in your mind what occurred at this dinner. I would encourage you to listen to an audio Bible and close your eyes and let your mind's eye create a scene of these events. Think about what this looked like. Consider how long this event may have gone on for the woman to create enough tears to wet the feet of Jesus. Listen to her cries. Watch and listen as she kisses His feet. Watch as the dust on His feet mix with her tears. (You will see at the end of Luke 7 that Simon had not washed Jesus' feet, so His feet were still dirty.) See her hair being used as a washrag to clean Jesus' feet. Then observe her take a flask and pour oil to anoint His feet. Smell the oil and dirt mixed with smells of dinner (not to mention the smell of self-righteousness). Then look around the room and see the disgust on the faces of the uppity religious snobs. Look at her hair after she is finished—tears, oil and dirt rubbed into her hair.

All of the senses are used here, but one thing you will not hear is this: You will not hear this woman utter one word. Yet her actions drew the highest praise from the Creator and Savior.

What Simon saw as disgusting, Jesus saw as the most beautiful picture of gratitude and love.

Let's look at what Simon saw but didn't see.

Look at how Simon sees the woman. Simon was repulsed by this woman and her actions. It tells you that he knew about this woman before she ever came into the house. It is clear that Simon did not care for her soul. Simon had no compassion for this woman in need of God's grace.

Look at how Simon sees Jesus. Simon saw himself as the judge of Jesus. Jesus isn't really the kind of prophet He should be, because He should know what kind of woman was touching him (Luke 7:39). We'll discuss more about this later, but Simon dishonored Jesus by not providing the customary and basic hospitality of the day (washing feet, anointing oil, greeting with a kiss).

Look at how Simon sees himself. According to Jesus' parable, Simon is the sort of person who really didn't see any need for God's forgiveness. He saw himself as having little sin debt. In his eyes, he was above Jesus and the woman.

"Simon, I have something to say to you."

Think about that. Jesus didn't confront him right away with "I know what you are thinking." Jesus did do that on other occasions. But here, Jesus' approach was to tell a parable, a method He frequently used to teach the unbelieving and hypocritical. His goal is to reshape Simon's vision and help him come to the right conclusion on his own.

Jesus, with divine vision, asked Simon to "see" this woman in a different light. The Lord of the universe shined the spotlight on this woman, not to rebuke and shame her publicly for her wickedness, but to draw public notice to what an amazing example of repentance, faith, gratitude and love she had shown.

His parable is basic, but powerful. Two men owe debts, 50 and 500 denarii. 500 days' wages versus 50 days. Think of what would take you a year and a half to work off compared to less than two months. Which person is going to be more thankful for the forgiveness of the debt?

> When they could not pay, he canceled the debt of both.
> Now which of them will love him more? (Luke 7:42)

Which of them will love him more? Which person will show the most gratitude?

This parable was used to open Simon's eyes to himself first. Only when Simon saw himself through heaven's vision could he ever begin to see this woman properly. Jesus did it in such a way as to have Simon answer the question, and then lead into really "seeing" this woman in a way Simon had never considered.

Contrast the sinful woman with Simon the Pharisee:

- She saw Jesus as the only hope for canceling that great debt of sin. Simon saw Jesus as a fraud because of His interaction with this woman.
- She sat below Jesus, at his feet. Simon sat in his seat above Jesus.
- She was overwhelmingly grateful and full of love for the gift given to her by Jesus. Simon clearly was not grateful because he didn't see himself as a sinner in the first place.
- She knew who Jesus was and came to Him for forgiveness. Simon knew who Jesus was and probably invited Him to dinner to find a fault in Him.
- She demonstrated the hospitality, love, and kindness that Simon should have shown. Simon didn't wash Jesus' feet, he didn't even give Jesus water to do it Himself. He didn't greet Jesus with a customary kiss on the cheek. He didn't anoint Jesus' head as a sign of blessing and honor.

These carefully chosen words of the Master Teacher accomplished several things. He rebuked Simon's hypocrisy and lack of love and hospitality. Jesus also showed to Simon and to all in the room what type of follower He is truly seeking. Through these words, Jesus gave great encouragement and hope to this beautiful woman of faith. She was comforted and reassured by Jesus that she was forgiven of all her sins, which were many. He honored her at this dinner in front of all who looked upon her with disdain.

—*Lesson 3 Discussion*—

1. What does it look and sound like today when we view others around us like Simon saw this woman?

2. How will this teaching reshape our spiritual vision as we look into the mirror and as we look out at others around us?

Lesson 4
Seeing a Woman Who Did What She Could

Mary, Sister of Martha, and Lazarus—
John 12:2–8; Matt. 26:6–13; Mark 14:3–9

"Wherever the gospel is preached in the whole world, what this woman has done will be told as a memorial to her." (Matthew 26:13)

CAN YOU IMAGINE doing something that impressed Jesus, the Creator of the Universe? Jesus is God in the flesh, the very One who said, "Let there be light … and it was so." He calmed the stormy seas of Galilee, cast out demons, made the lame walk, gave sight to the blind, turned water into wine, and with just a word, He called Lazarus from the tomb. What could a person ever do to impress Jesus?

What we find in the gospel accounts is a record of such an event that deeply touched the heart and soul of the Son of God. A woman named Mary, sister of Lazarus and Martha, took a flask containing very expensive oil and poured it over Jesus, anointing His head and feet. She even wiped off the oil with her own hair. This tender act of faith and devotion moved Jesus to declare to His disciples that her deed would be told throughout the world. For 2000 years, in every nation on earth, Mary's example is shared when the gospel is proclaimed.

Mary is known in Scripture by her deeds, not by her words. We only have one recorded statement of hers in the Bible in John 11:32. What we do find, though, is that every time in Scripture she is mentioned, she is at the feet of Jesus.

So, at this supper in John 12, which happens shortly before the crucifixion of Jesus, we see Mary at His feet, but why? We are not left to wonder, because Jesus told the disciples why Mary did what she did. She anointed Jesus in preparation and anticipation of His coming burial. Mary understood, by her continued devotion to His teachings, that Jesus would soon die. She decided to use this very valuable oil as a sacrifice and an honor to anoint her Lord and Savior before His death, not afterwards. Mary appears to have understood by faith what many of Jesus' closest disciples failed to grasp.

Certainly, it is not a stretch to add that she also was filled with tremendous gratitude for the recent raising of her brother Lazarus from the dead (John 11). Lazarus was sitting there at the table!

However, not everyone at the supper was as impressed by Mary's deed as Jesus. In fact, He was the only one who saw her deed as a positive thing. The disciples were "indignant," according to Mark's account. Mary was scolded and criticized sharply by the other disciples for wasting such valuable oil. They had better ways she could have served Jesus and offered her gift. They all had affixed their own value to the oil, and they all had better use for it. After all, this oil was worth the equivalent of 300 days' wages (You do the math!). The most vocal of the opposition came from Judas, whom John noted was only concerned about the money because he was a thief. He valued what he could steal out of the disciples' money bag.

Thankfully, Jesus was there to give divine perspective. Sadly, there are times among God's people that some are discouraged out of faith-filled service by hypercritical and overly opinionated believers. Death and life are in the power of the tongue, Solomon once wrote. The disciples were harping on Mary's poor judgment, while Jesus would ensure that her example was forever etched in the memories of Christians for thousands of years to come!

Jesus said, "Leave her alone. Why do you trouble her? She has done a good work for Me." His words for the "righteous" were to back off and stand down, and those words are just as valuable today. We often have far too many words for how others should or should not serve God, and how they should or should not use their gifts in service to God. That really reveals more about us and the condition of our own hearts than it does the people we seek to correct and change. The words of the Master Teacher show us here that we can often do more harm than good by trying to make others serve God in the way we deem acceptable.

It is not my intention to say that we ignore doctrinal error or overlook false teaching, because that is not even in the context here. Jesus Himself often corrected those who promoted false doctrines. What Mary did was not wrong, even though the disciples were fully convinced that she was. This passage can serve as a reminder for us to be sure we have truth on our tongues and love in our hearts before we start trying to correct others' service to Jesus.

My goal in pointing out Jesus' words is for you to consider that Mary's gift had nothing whatsoever to do with the other disciples. This was between her and Jesus, and it should stay there. Her act of faith, her generosity, and her sacrifice did not alter their lives or circumstances in any way. Frankly, it was none of their business, and that is exactly what Jesus told them. The apostle Paul put it this way, when he urged believers to "lead a quiet life, to mind your own business, and to work with your own hands, as we commanded you" (1 Thessalonians 4:11).

If someone has a gift for God, then be the person who fans the flames of encouragement. Be very cautious about the criticism and suggestion parade for how she could do it better. Tread lightly when entering discussions about how someone can better improve his or her service to Jesus. Are you trying to shape people into your own image or are you trying to help encourage people to be conformed to Christ's image?

Jesus said, "For you have the poor with you always, and whenever you wish you may do them good; but Me you do not have always" (Matthew 26:11). There will always be good works to do. There will always be needs to fill. Whenever we desire, there will always be some place to direct our efforts. We will never run out of opportunities to serve our fellow man. We can at any time exhaust our bodies and bank accounts helping those with needs, but this moment in time for Mary was specifically for her to focus on her Lord and to honor Him directly with this gift. This meant that the opportunity and the money that could have been spent elsewhere in good works was poured out upon Jesus.

And that's okay.

Jesus said, 'She has done what she could.' This sentence from Jesus can serve as an encouragement for every person who walks with Him. Every person can only do for Jesus what he or she can.

Not every person is in the same situation or circumstance in life. However, each of us is created in God's own image (Genesis 1:26–27) and we've been blessed by God with a unique set of talents, personality, perspective, and opportunities that we can offer to Jesus. Ask for God's help to see your own value to Him. Pray for clarity to see with His eyes how He has uniquely blessed you with gifts, abilities, and opportunities. Come to the Father for power to overcome the temptation to compare yourself with how others serve Jesus (2 Corinthians 10:12). May God's Spirit lift you up from the heavy burden of others' criticism so that you can walk with renewed strength and soar like an eagle. Talk with other godly-minded brothers and sisters to get encouragement on how you can offer your gifts to the Lord.

Mary did what she could for Jesus. You, with God's blessing, can offer your special gift too.

—*Lesson 4 Discussion*—

1. Think of a woman in your life who "did what she could" for Jesus. How did she do what she could?

2. Why do we criticize others so much, and how can we change this part of our character to be more like Jesus? What does it sound like when we attempt to justify ourselves in our criticism of others' service to God?

3. What can *you* do for Jesus? What are your talents and opportunities God has given you? How will you pour out your gratitude to Jesus?

Lesson 5
Seeing a Woman Who Was Distracted

Martha, sister of Mary and Lazarus—
Luke 10:38–42; John 11:1–6, 17–28

"Hey, Jesus! Don't you see I'm busy working my fingers to the bone here in the kitchen all by myself? Don't you care that I'm feverishly trying to take care of all these guests? Mary is not helping me; I mean … she isn't doing anything. She is just sitting there on the floor listening to you. Why can't you tell her to get her tail over here in the kitchen to help me? You see, Jesus, my "ministry" is service and hospitality, and I'm trying my best to make sure that everything is just right so everyone's needs are met. But Jesus, I can't do this all alone. There are meals to prepare, breads to bake, tables to set, drinks to fill, and dishes to do. Tell her to get in here and do something!"

The above words are merely my paraphrase, so please read Luke 10:38–42 to see how the Holy Spirit through Luke records the actual conversation between Martha and Jesus. We are going to dive into this passage and learn some things about Martha. We'll learn something about ourselves along the way.

"Martha welcomed Him into her house."

Martha was hospitable, that was her gift and her passion, and that is a good thing. In fact, God expects every single believer to be hospitable and to serve others. As God's people we are all to use our homes and resources to share with others, especially with the less fortunate (Romans 12:13; Hebrews 13:2, 16).

Martha was a servant, a doer, and it seems that she had a very practical, no-nonsense personality about her. These are great character and personality traits and are very useful in the kingdom of God. She wanted to make sure that Jesus and the other guests were comfortable and were well-fed. This is not the only time we find Martha serving guests and using her gifts of hospitality. In our previous lesson, when we looked at the occasion of Mary anointing Jesus before His death, do you remember what Martha was doing during this supper? She was serving (John 12:2)! We are very thankful for the Martha's in our lives. They get the job done, don't they?

So, what's the problem? Isn't Martha doing what she was supposed to be doing? Is that not what Jesus had been preaching about all along? Even Jesus said to be greatest in His kingdom, you had to be the servant of all. At one point He asked His disciples, "For who is greater, he who sits at the table, or he who serves? Is it not he who sits at the table? Yet I am among you as the One who serves" (Luke 22:27). Martha had that very heart, the heart of a servant, so Jesus was by no means correcting her for trying to serve others and to take care of others' needs.

"Martha was distracted with much serving." (Luke 10:40)

What did Luke just say? What was distracting Martha? Much serving. You see, Martha was not being pulled away by worldly pursuits; she was just trying to be a servant to others. She was so involved in serving that she lost perspective on the reason for the gathering. The dinner became the focus instead of the feast of teaching Jesus was offering. This is a vital point in the text here. She was not getting distracted with immoral things and indulgence in sinful pleasure; she was getting sidetracked while using her gifts and talents that God had given her. The Scripture records that these things had become a "distraction" for her.

"Martha, Martha, you are worried and troubled about many things." Luke 10:41 Martha, Martha. Remember that Jesus loved Martha just as much as He loved Mary and Lazarus (John 11:5). Martha wanted more than anything to please her Lord, but she just needed to fix her glasses.

When you read John 11:20–27, you will find that Martha had great faith in the power of Jesus. She had a strong conviction that the dead, including her brother Lazarus, would rise again on the Last Day. Consider her confession of faith in Jesus when she said, "Yes, Lord, I believe that You are the Christ, the Son of God, who is to come into the world." She knew He was the promised Savior, the promised King (Messiah), and God in the flesh. Her confession demonstrates an understanding equal to that of Peter (Matthew 16:16).

Martha was a dedicated servant to Jesus, but she lost her focus. Jesus, in His tenderness and patience, called Martha back to reality and perspective.

Here is the reality—Martha was worried and troubled over a lot of stuff. She was worried about the guests. She was troubled over all the preparations. She was worked up over what she considered to be Mary's lack of involvement. And here's the kicker—she was really bothered by her assumption that Jesus did not even seem to care that Mary had left her alone to serve all these guests!

Here is the perspective—Mary had chosen the good part. Mary was not lazy. Mary was not inhospitable. Mary was not less interested in taking care of others. She, as Jesus said, had chosen to focus on the most important and pressing thing at the time, and that was to listen to what Jesus was saying. Both Mary and Martha "approached" Jesus, but for very different reasons. Mary sat at His feet to listen to what He had to say, but Martha wanted to tell Jesus what to do.

"She approached Him and said, 'Lord, do You not care that my sister has left me to serve alone? Therefore tell her to help me'" (Luke 10:40). When we become "worried and troubled over many things," we can fall into the same trap Martha did. Martha became the standard of judgment for Mary, and she even assumed that Jesus would agree with her assessment of the situation. She could not figure out why Jesus would not order Mary to get in the kitchen. Like Martha, we can begin to view our gifts and level of involvement as the standard of judgment for others.

For example:

- You go visit someone in the hospital or take food to a shut-in and wonder why every Christian cannot find the time to do what you are doing. I mean, how hard is it to get a meal together and go visit with dear sister Smith?

- You are cleaning the church building and wonder why every person is not as diligent and dedicated as you are. You wouldn't have such a hard time cleaning if the family the week before would have "done their job."
- You stay up extra late or get up extra early to make sure that your Bible class lesson is completed and come to Bible study and see so many adults with nothing done at all in their workbooks. Some have blank pages and blank expressions, some even forgot their books. Why can't they just spend more time preparing at home?
- You say to yourself, "Good grief! There comes the Jones family again. Late as usual to service. Running in at the last minute. I mean, come on, Sunday morning comes the same time every week. Why can't they get it together and set the alarm clock a half hour earlier?"
- If you are a wife and mother, sometimes you may wish that your kids or husband would see things around the house with your eyes. Maybe then they would appreciate all that you do, and they would finally get their act together and help you.

Martha saw herself as alone when that was the furthest thing from the truth. Elijah, a prophet in the Old Testament, once saw himself as all alone, and God had to remind him that there were thousands of other dedicated followers all around him (1 Kings 19). Just because someone is not focused on the same task as you at the moment does not mean that he or she does not care as much as you do. Just because someone is not as involved at the same level in a certain activity as you are does not mean that they are somehow lazy with God.

When we get troubled and worried over many things, our joy of serving and the blessing of using our gifts for Jesus get replaced with bitterness and resentment. We start grumbling about the work and complaining (even to God) about others. It just becomes a job, a grind, and we really don't like doing it anymore.

Jesus knows our tendency to get distracted while doing good works, and He is acutely aware of how easily we lose our focus and begin to grumble against God and others. That is why so many Scriptures are devoted to this very thing.

- Do not grumble against one another (James 5:9).
- Be hospitable... without grumbling (1 Peter 4:9).
- Do all things without complaining... (Philippians 2:14).
- And let us not grow weary while doing good, for in due season we shall reap if we do not lose heart (Galatians 4:9).

So then, what is a person to do when he or she falls into this trap? What further words of encouragement did Jesus have for Martha?

"But one thing is needed, and Mary has chosen that good part, which will not be taken away from her" (Luke 10:42). Mary took time to focus on the one thing that mattered, so therefore it meant that some very important things had to be set aside for the moment. Jesus was not condemning Martha in any way for being a servant, He was encouraging her to see Mary in a positive light. He was giving Martha permission to set her apron aside for a moment and to focus on the one thing that truly mattered—His words of life and salvation.

If people had to eat a little later, it was fine. If the guests did not have everything they wanted for supper, it would not be the end of the world. Jesus seemed to have little concern here if the house was immaculate and spotless. Who was in that house that day and what was said mattered more than who was working and what was being served. All too often we get caught up in the jobs and the ministry and forget the people and the perspective.

Mary was Mary and Martha was Martha. Jesus did not expect Martha to be Mary, but Jesus expected Martha to use her talents in His service while keeping focused on the one thing that mattered.

—Lesson 5 Discussion—

1. What are some indicators that we are distracted with much serving?

2. How do we balance service (using our gifts) with sitting at the feet of Jesus?

3. Could we become too much of a Mary, and forget to be a Martha? Are there times when Bible study isn't what God wants us to do, but rather getting out there and helping people?

Lesson 6
Seeing a Woman
Who Touched Jesus' Garment

The Woman with the Blood Issue—
Matthew 9:20–22; Mark 5:25–34; Luke 8:42–48

"I'M SORRY, MRS. JONES, but there is nothing more we can do. We have tried everything humanly possible, but we cannot cure your condition. The best we can do is make you comfortable for your remaining days and ease your passing."

Words like these are sadly part of our everyday language. Each day, people around the world are told by doctors that there is nothing more they can do. Sometimes those doctors are incorrect in their diagnoses, but many times they are right. Physicians are amazing people who have invented and administered incredible life-saving treatments, but we are often reminded that they are only human and there is only so much they can do. When we stare the doctor in the eyes and hear those painful words that all options have been exhausted, we know very quickly that we also are only human.

Hopeless. Desperate. The only prospects are weakness, pain, and death.

The gospel writers tell of many such people in the days of Jesus who suffered from various incurable diseases, but we will focus on one particular woman who was commended by Jesus for her touch of faith.

Luke's description of this woman:

Now a woman, having a flow of blood for twelve years, who had spent all her livelihood on physicians and could not be healed by any. (Luke 8:42)

Mark's description of this woman:

Now a certain woman had a flow of blood for twelve years and had suffered many things from many physicians. She had spent all that she had and was no better, but rather grew worse." (Mark 5:25–26)

Do you see this woman? Maybe you see it in your own physical ailments. Maybe you have seen it in others as you watched an incurable disorder slowly destroy the body and steal your dear loved one away from you. You would be hard pressed to find an occasion in life when you are more powerless and without options than when death is calling, and you can do nothing to stop it.

We must appreciate the hopelessness of this poor woman's condition. Mark and Luke record that she had spent every dime she had in paying various physicians to attempt myriad healing measures. Mark notes that she had "suffered" many things from many physicians. They were trying to help her, but the medicines and treatments only made her worse. She was anemic. She was weak and tired. She got a second opinion. She got a third opinion. Fourth. Fifth. "Please somebody help me! Please, somebody make this bleeding stop! Can't you see I'm dying? This has been going on for 12 years, time is running out!"

Her condition made her unclean spiritually. This affected her worship. She would not be allowed in the temple because of this. There were many rumors about certain "diseases." Some would have added the burden that God was punishing her for some secret sexual sins in her past. Sick. Helpless. Unable to go to worship. Rumors. Questionable past. No one to help her.

"When she heard about Jesus…" These are words of light, deliverance and hope that fall upon the ears of this dying woman. Jesus of Nazareth is the miracle healer. He is casting out demons, making the lame walk, and causing the blind to see. Crowds are coming from all over Israel, and He is immediately healing diseases of every kind. There seemingly is no impossible condition for Him to fix.

She may have heard how Jesus cured the incurable. He healed lepers. No one could do that. He cast out demons. No one could do that. The blind received their sight and the lame walked, some for the first time in their life. This Jesus was doing what even doctors could not do. She heard about Jesus.

"Yes, this Jesus can heal me," she said to herself. "I'm going to get to Jesus."

We also have to appreciate that this was no simple task. Thousands of people were surrounding Jesus continually. Mark noted earlier in his gospel that the crowds were pressing about Jesus so much that they almost crushed Him (Mark 3:7–10). When Jesus went into a house, people crammed into the house to the point that there was not even room near the door. Some even crawled up on top of the roof one time and tore a panel off to lower their friend down to Jesus (Mark 2:1–12). It is clear that this woman with the blood issue was not the only one with a desperate situation. In fact, at the very moment she was trying to reach out to touch Jesus, He was on his way to heal Jairus' dying daughter. How could a weakened woman possibly push through the crowds to talk to Jesus? How could she possibly secure her moment with Jesus in order for Him to consider her condition?

This is where her remarkable faith in Jesus shines brightly.

"For she said, 'If only I may touch His clothes, I shall be made well'" (Matthew 9:21). Her faith and understanding had grown to the point that she only had to touch the hem of His garment as He passed by, and His power would heal her. She had convinced herself through faith that she did not have to get Jesus' attention personally that day. She didn't have to have an appointment. She didn't have to pay anything. She didn't have to have Him stop and take some time for a personal one-on-one consultation. She just had to get one touch of His clothes as He walked by, and she would be made well. Friends, that is pure, one hundred percent faith! Just a quick touch, that's all it takes. No one will notice. No one will know.

I cannot imagine how physically difficult it must have been for this woman in such a weakened condition to push through the crowds, but I believe that God made it happen for her. He gave her the strength and the opportunity to reach out to Jesus and touch His clothes.

Her flow of blood stopped. Jesus stopped too.

By the way, have you ever tried to stop and stand still in a crowd of thousands that is all going one direction? There is a sense of urgency taking place. Jairus' daughter was dying. This was a 9-1-1 situation. This was not the time for chit-chat. Jesus was being hurried along.

"Who touched Me?" (Mark 5:30b) Only Jesus, Creator of heaven and earth, could say such a thing. His question, considering the huge crowds and how they thronged Him, sounded almost insane to His disciples. Notice that in Luke's account, Peter is singled out as asking Jesus, "Master, the multitudes throng and press You, and You say, 'Who touched Me?'" (Mark 5:31) A reasonable and valid question, don't you think? Can you imagine how silly Jesus' question must have sounded to everyone at that moment?

"Somebody touched Me, for I perceived power going out from Me." (Luke 8:46) All kinds of people were touching, grabbing, shoving, and pulling on Jesus that day, which was an everyday occurrence for Him. However, Jesus recognized something different and very special about the touch that came from this desperate, dying woman—the touch of faith.

> Now when the woman saw that she was not hidden, she came trembling; and falling down before Him, she declared to Him in the presence of all the people the reason she had touched Him and how she was healed immediately. (Luke 8:47)

She was not hidden. Jesus, the disciples, Jairus (whose mind is on his dying daughter), and the entire crowd that day were now staring right at her. The spotlight was on her, and she fell down trembling before Jesus and told Him in front of everyone what had just happened.

You know, Jesus didn't have to stop, did He? He is God! He knew her condition before she ever came to Him that day. He knew what faith was building within her. He knew what her plans were that day. In fact, given the situation, most of us would have gone on to Jairus' house first. This woman had this problem for 12 years. Another hour is not going to change anything. Plus, Jairus was a synagogue official. He was important. This woman to the human eye was insignificant and broke. But to Jesus, she was just as important as Jairus' dying daughter. He felt her touch that brought forth the healing power from His Divine Spirit to heal her dying body.

He could have saved her the embarrassment and fear of being singled out, yet He did not. He could have saved Jairus an incredible amount of anxiety at this point; remember that Jairus is anxiously waiting for Jesus to get to his house. He could have saved Peter the embarrassment of once again opening his mouth and inserting his foot. The Master Teacher takes yet another opportunity for a teaching moment on what true saving faith looks like.

Jesus stopped that day to commend this woman in front of everyone for her amazing demonstration of faith in God. He could have let her have her own personal victory and go on her way rejoicing, but it was vital for all present that day and all who read the gospels even today to see the Divine spotlight shine upon this very weak, yet very mighty woman of faith.

> And He said to her, "Daughter, your faith has made you well.
> Go in peace, and be healed of your affliction." (Mark 5:34)

She went home that day with a peace that she had never felt before. She knew that only Jesus had the answers for her. For over 12 years, her life consisted of false hope followed by devastating disappointments, but not today with Jesus.

Her faith made her well, but what kind of faith did she have?

1. She had a faith that was based upon hearing about Jesus. The apostle Paul teaches us that "faith comes through hearing." Romans 10:17 The reports about the mighty deeds of Jesus rang in her ears and it produced a faith that was personal. Not only could Jesus save—He could save her.

2. Her faith was affected by her condition. She knew that there was no hope to be offered by anyone or anything. She was bankrupt—physically, emotionally, and financially. If anyone was going to deliver her, it was going to be Jesus. He was her last and best opportunity. He was her only hope. One reason people today cannot be saved from their sins by the Great Physician is that they do not know they are lost. Jesus said, "Blessed are the poor in spirit, for theirs is the kingdom of heaven." Only

those who are spiritually bankrupt can see Jesus as the only name by which they will be saved. Sometimes we do not look in the right mirror to see our true spiritual condition before the Judge of all the earth.

3. She had a faith that shaped her understanding. Hebrews 11:3 says, "By faith we understand" certain things. Our faith forms the foundation for our thinking about our lives and about God's power and His work within our lives. Our faith becomes the lens through which we see ourselves and the world. We see God differently. We see ourselves differently. This woman's faith molded the way she thought, and her faith sculpted her conclusion that all she had to do was get close enough to touch His clothes and she would be made well.

4. Her faith produced action. James 2:14–26 teaches that "faith without works is dead". We demonstrate our faith in Jesus, and we truly let God know how much we think we need Him by how we live on a daily basis. Just like the men who let their friend down through the roof, Jesus "saw" the faith of this woman (Mark 2:5; 5:34). This kind of faith is manifested in a "there is nothing that is going to stop me from getting to Jesus" kind of mindset.

Do we have the faith of this woman? Do we see ourselves as hopeless, powerless, and desperate in our souls without the saving, life-giving blood of the Lamb of God? Do we truly recognize Jesus as the only One who can save us? Is that kind of faith witnessed in the way we live our daily lives?

Where could I go but to the Lord? Most likely we have tried to do everything we can on our own to make ourselves feel better inside, but we end up spiritually and morally destitute. We look up in despair for some glimmer of light and hope. Then we hear about Jesus, the Great Physician, and we reach up to Him in our frailty, and He lifts us up with His mighty, yet tender arm. With His own blood He cleanses us, and with His fullness and presence He fills that emptiness that we have tried to fill with all the wrong things. He didn't give us a temporary fix. He didn't mask the symptoms. He healed us… completely.

—Lesson 6 Discussion—

1. Many people were pressing about Jesus, but Jesus recognized the touch of faith. Does Jesus know our touch, or is ours just one of the crowd?

2. What are the "doctors" we go to today to try to make us feel better, but all they do is leave us worse? For example, Dr. Money, Dr. Fun, Dr. Things, etc.

Lesson 7
Seeing a Woman
Who Left Her Water Pot

The Samaritan Woman at the Well—John 4:1–42

THE WOMAN THEN LEFT HER WATER POT, went her way into the city, and said to the men, "Come, see a Man who told me all things that I ever did. Could this be the Christ?" Then they went out of the city and came to Him (John 4:28–30).

No man could ever give her what she received from Jesus that day.

She left her water pot.

This Samaritan came to Jacob's well as a woman with five broken marriages, mixed up doctrine, and a focus on earthly things. As she arrived at the well and saw this Jewish man sitting there asking her for a drink, the racial and religious tension between Jews and Samaritans was immediately made obvious. This would be no normal day for the Samaritan woman, because after a few moments with Jesus, she left her water pot, and instantly became a passionate witness to the Messiah. Because of her influence and testimony, a whole city of Samaritans came to hear and believe in Jesus.

What in the world did Jesus say or do that created such a dramatic change within her so quickly?

Jesus knew that she would wonder why He, being a Jew, would even speak to her. He knew her sinful past, including her string of divorces and broken relationships. He knew that she would think of the physical instead of the spiritual as He taught her. He was well aware of her mixed-up views on doctrine and worship. He also knew that He would be engaging in several "taboos" by going to speak with her.

But John recorded that Jesus "needed to go through Samaria." (John 4:4)

Jesus needed to go through Samaria.

Initially this statement may seem simply matter of fact. Jesus left Judea, which was in the southern part of Palestine, to travel north to Galilee, but on the way, He needed to travel through Samaria. Geographically, I could compare it to leaving Texas on my way to Florida on Interstate 10, but I need to make a stop in Louisiana. What's the big deal?

There is far more involved here than mere geographical convenience. Why is this decision of Jesus to go through Samaria so significant? We get a glimpse of it in John 4:9, when John records, "For the Jews have no dealings with the Samaritans."

When the New Testament begins, the gospels speak of people called Samaritans, noting how despised they were by the Jews. In fact, for a Jew to call someone a "Samaritan" was a nasty insult (John 8:48). Understand though, that the feeling was mutual—there were many Samaritans who wanted nothing to do with Jesus and refused to be hospitable to him. When this happened, James and John were ready to call down fire from heaven to burn them up (Luke 9:51–56)! Obviously, there was no love lost between these two groups of people. However, we do not find explanation in the gospels as to why there was such a long-standing animosity between Jews and Samaritans. Therefore, we need to take a moment to understand a little background on the Samaritans, their origin, and their relationship to the Jews.

How the Samaritans came to be.

The very existence of the Samaritans served as a painful reminder of a dark chapter in Israel's history. In 722 BC, the kingdom of Assyria came and besieged the city of Samaria, which was capital of the northern kingdom of Israel (2 Kings 17). Many inhabitants of Samaria and the surrounding area were led away into captivity. This happened because the nation of Israel, the people who were the descendants of Abraham and the covenant people of God, had left their Lord and served every god they could find, and participated in every abominable practice imaginable. Since they stubbornly refused to listen to God's pleas through His prophets to return to Him, there was no remedy but to punish them harshly and send them away into pagan nations to live. In turn, the Assyrians brought people from many other nations and made them live in Samaria and the neighboring cities. What resulted was an intermarrying of these pagan people with the people of Israel who remained in the land. Eventually, this mixed-bred group called "Samaritans" emerged who "feared the Lord, yet served their idols." (2 Kings 17:41)

The Samaritans picked their own mountain on which to worship God, which was Mount Gerizim. They chose to only accept the first five books of Scripture (Genesis through Deuteronomy). They opposed the Jews who had returned to Jerusalem from Babylonian captivity as the Jews sought to rebuild the city and the temple. Over a hundred years before Jesus was born, some zealous Jews went and destroyed the Samaritan's temple on Mount Gerizim. Again, clearly no love lost between Jews and Samaritans.

Racial, moral, doctrinal, and ethnic differences abounded between Jews and Samaritans, and there seemed to be little hope that this would ever change.

"The Jews have no dealings with the Samaritans." (John 4:9)

Many Jews would go out of their way to avoid Samaritans, but not Jesus on this day. He needed to go through Samaria. Why? There were precious souls to reach with the gospel, beginning with the Samaritan woman at Jacob's well. The fields, Jesus said that day to His disciples, were "white unto harvest." "For the Son of Man is come to seek and to save that which was lost." (Luke 19:10)

So, knowing the racial and religious climate, and knowing this woman's checkered past, it is stunning, shocking, and even scandalous that Jesus would even speak to her.

So, what did Jesus do for the Samaritan Woman that day? How did He affect such great change within her in such a short time?

He treated her as someone with eternal value (John 4:6–9).

Women in many cultures and times have been oppressed by men, and it is certainly evidenced in the pages of Scripture. They were often considered expendable and of no importance (John 8:1–12). Livestock were treated with more concern than daughters of Abraham (Luke 13:10–17). Heartless husbands cast their wives aside, abandoning them for other women (Malachi 2:13–16). They were used as objects for sexual gratification, simply a piece of meat for man's pleasure (Matthew 5:28; 2 Samuel 13). Their word was not trusted (Luke 24:10–11; Mark 16:9–11), nor were they considered by many men to be equals (John 4:27). There are many men in Scripture, such as men like Boaz and Joseph, who did not treat women this way, but they are the exception, sadly, and not the rule. Even Jesus said that Moses gave certain instructions about marriage because of the hardness of many men's hearts (Matthew 19:1–9).

It is crucial for us to see how exceptionally different and unique Jesus is in how He views, speaks to, and treats women.

Jesus, the Creator of women, regarded women as image-bearers of God and as joint-heirs of the eternal blessings of His kingdom (Genesis 1:26–27; 1 Peter 3:7). He saw their inherent value and potential, and He often employed them in His ministry. The Samaritan woman at Jacob's well is a powerful demonstration of what God sees in women.

Notice that both the Samaritan woman and even Jesus' disciples were shocked that He would dare speak to her—shocked for many reasons. Jesus spoke to a woman in public. Respectable Jewish men just didn't do that. What would people say? Not only was she a woman, she was also a Samaritan. She, to the Jewish mind, was a dog, and even her vessel with which she came to draw water was unclean. Not only was she a woman and a Samaritan, she had also been married five times and now she is shacking up with another man. I can hear Simon the Pharisee from Luke 7 saying, "This Man, if He were a prophet, would know what manner of woman this is ... for she is a sinner." (Luke 7:39)

Why would Jesus engage in so many social and religious taboos? Because He looked into her soul and saw something very precious. Through His divine vision, He saw what she could become, not who she currently was.

This should be a wake-up call for all men to see women as Jesus Christ sees them. It should also be a daily reminder for all Christians to see everyone around us as precious souls in need of God's salvation, no matter where they come from, what they look like or what they have done. It should also lift up the hearts of women of all ages to see how truly valuable and special they are to God in heaven. As image-bearers of God, ladies should have the expectation that they deserve to be treated as valuable.

He showed her a true relationship (John 4:10–26). How many times had she been married? Five times. How was marriage working out for her? We do not know why she was divorced multiple times, but it is clear that she did not have a fulfilling relationship with a man as God originally intended (Genesis 2:18–24).

What do you think are the reasons for Jesus bringing up her past failed relationships? One reason would be to demonstrate His own identity as the Messiah. He did this by showing divine knowledge of her marital condition. Another reason for Jesus bringing up the past would be to connect her past to the living water which she had just requested. Only Jesus could rescue her from her sinful past and give her a new fulfilling life. Thirdly, she needed a new relationship, and no man on earth could give it to her. Physical companionship is not what she needed. Marriage, though a gift from God, is not what completes us—Jesus completes us (Colossians 2:10). People often run through relationships like they do paper towels because they are seeking something that will never be found in human companionship. She was a broken woman, and no man, no matter how genuinely he tried, could heal her brokenness.

Why do we see so many people going from one failed relationship to another? What are people looking for that will never be found in all those partners? What we think we are looking for, just like the woman at the well, may not be what we really need. For whatever reason she went from man to man, and it didn't last. Now she is asking Jesus for "living water," thinking on the physical—She thought He had some inside scoop on a great way to always have fresh water. However, Jesus wasn't the Culligan man, He was going to save her soul and truly fulfill her so that she would never thirst again. "The Lord is my Shepherd, I shall not want." (Psalm 23:1a)

He gave her a new purpose (John 4:28–29).

After this short conversation with Jesus, a woman's life was forever changed! Consider the power that Jesus placed within her by treating her with great value and by giving her a new relationship. She blossomed immediately, springing into life, changing instantly from damaged goods to a soul-saving machine. Only Jesus can affect that kind of change in someone.

The purpose of the woman was directly tied to the identity of Jesus. I encourage you to go back over John 4 and note how her understanding of His identity grew. At first, she saw Him as just another Jewish man. Then she asked Him if He was greater than their father Jacob. After He told everything about her marriage history, she "perceived" that He was a prophet. Finally, Jesus led her to the ultimate understanding of His identity as the Messiah, the Savior of the World, and King of all Kings. Based upon this understanding, her purpose in life instantly changed. She went into that city armed with very little information, but with a powerful testimony about the Messiah.

And many of the Samaritans of that city believed in Him because of the word of the woman who testified, "He told me all that I ever did." … And many more believed because of His own word. Then they said to the woman, "Now we believe, not because of what you said, for we ourselves have heard Him and we know that this is indeed the Christ, the Savior of the world" (John 4:39–42).

Because of the word of the woman.

Please do not underestimate the influence you can have on countless others around you. You don't have to have a Bible degree and a flawless past to tell someone about Jesus. Because of your influence and your encouraging words, you can change the course of those around you for generations to come. This Samaritan woman's words about Jesus changed the lives of many people in that village. Through the power of Jesus, you can do the same.

—*Lesson 7 Discussion*—

1. Can you think of those around you (or maybe yourself) who is like this Samaritan woman at the well?

2. Why is it important for us to remember that Jesus is the one who completes us, and no other person can do that for us?

3. Think of the effect this one broken Samaritan woman had on a whole city of people? Can you do the same?

Lesson 8
Seeing a Woman
Who Married Mr. Worthless

Abigail, wife of Nabal—1 Samuel 25

A ROTTEN SCOUNDREL and a righteous warrior are at a deadly point of conflict, and an attractive woman with a good head on her shoulders is caught in between the two. Wow, that first sentence might sound like a trailer for a great drama, but this action-packed romantic drama is within Scripture. As we journey into 1 Samuel 25 together, let us first take some time to consider the three main characters.

David

He is a shepherd who had a heart tuned in to God. He was called by the Lord and anointed to be the next king of Israel because God refused to let the kingdom of Saul stand. This was a direct result of Saul's rebellion and pride (see 1 Samuel 13 and 15). While Saul was still king, David rose in popularity among the people, especially after he slew the giant, Goliath. This bred great jealousy, paranoia, and hatred on the part of King Saul, stirring him to pursue David all over Israel in attempts to kill him.

During this time of running for his life, David showed great trust in God, as well as patience and humility. When David had the opportunity to attack the Philistines, he first inquired of the Lord's will (1 Samuel 23:2–4). He also showed great restraint when he had the perfect chance to kill King Saul, but he refused because he knew it was sinful to strike the Lord's anointed (1 Samuel 24). David had been unlawfully chased, falsely accused, and shamefully treated, and he was the victim of attempted murder on more than one occasion. In fact, King Saul had 85 priests and the whole city of Nob slaughtered because they gave refuge and assistance to David. David had several opportunities to take vengeance into his own hands and refused every time.

However, just like every human, David had his snapping point.

David and his loyal soldiers were fleeing and hiding from King Saul, but at the same time they provided security for Nabal's shepherds while in the area. As was customary, they requested a reasonable gratuity or "tip" for their services. They just wanted a meal on a feast day. We will see that Nabal, a worthless scoundrel of a businessman, seemed to find the right straw to put on the camel's back, and David was about to massacre a whole family and corporation. He is about to do something in his rage that he would forever regret. Who will talk some sense into him? Well, it was not Nabal.

Nabal

Nothing good is said of this man in Scripture. The only redeeming thing he had going for him was his wife, who we will discuss in just a moment. Nabal owned a large livestock business. He, like David, was of the tribe of Judah. He was "harsh and evil in his doings" according to verse 3. However, he got his riches, it certainly was not from being an honest businessman with integrity and class. Brown-Driver-Brigg's defines harsh as hard, severe, cruel, stubborn, and fierce. In 1 Samuel 25:10, Nabal showed great condescension and a serious lack of gratitude for David and his men when he accused David of being a traitor to King Saul's throne. He scorned and reviled David and his men, repaying them evil for good (1 Samuel 25:14, 21). His arrogance and self-absorption are made readily apparent in 1 Samuel 25:11 when Nabal used "I," "me," or "my" seven times. Nabal was in love with Nabal. Do you know anybody like that?

To further illustrate what kind of character Nabal was, think of how freely willing his own slaves were in speaking to their master's wife about him. To talk bad about your boss is one thing, but to go to his wife is completely another! Yet, we see in the text that they knew they could talk to her, and they knew she would do something to remedy the situation. It is safe to say that this is not the first time they came to Abigail about Nabal.

Nabal was called by his own servants a "scoundrel" (1 Samuel 25:17) which means "a son of Belial." The name "Belial" is from two words which together mean worthless, of no value at all. To call someone a "Son of Belial" was basically the same as calling him Satan. Nabal's own name meant "fool," and even Abigail freely confessed that he lived up to his name (see 1 Samuel 25:25). It makes you wonder what his parents were thinking in naming him "fool." Nabal was impossible. He was unapproachable. Nobody could talk to him, and nobody wanted to, either. To whom shall those suffering because of Nabal go for help?

Abigail

The Scripture describes Abigail, the wife of Nabal, as "a woman of good understanding and beautiful appearance." The English Standard Version translates this as "discerning and beautiful." She was pretty—she looked good on the outside, but more importantly she was very wise. One of the first things I wondered when reading 1 Samuel 25:3 is how a woman like that ended up with such a jerk. Maybe it was an arranged marriage, but there are other possible explanations, and the Bible simply does not tell us how or why they ended up together. The reality is, she is married to a worthless scoundrel, and she has to deal with what she has been given.

The word "discerning" means having good sense and insight. Abigail was attractive on the outside, but what saved the day (and a lot of lives) here was her discernment. She knew what to say, how to say it, and when to say it. She knew how to approach someone, but she also knew when to leave someone alone (1 Samuel 25:19, 36). Because of her discretion, she took a volatile and deadly situation and diffused it with calm reasoning and tender care.

A word spoken in due season.

"Death and life are in the power of the tongue," the Proverb writer said (Proverbs 18:21), and that truth is demonstrated here with Abigail. David made an oath to his men that together they would slaughter every male of Nabal's household by morning light (1 Samuel 25:22, 34). What stood in between that promise and its eventuality was the well-placed words and careful actions of Abigail.

She kept her cool.

How crucial is it for us to keep our cool when others' tempers are flaring? Ask Abigail! The Bible says, "Whoever has no rule over his own spirit is like a city broken down, without walls" (Proverbs 25:28). A city without walls in those days was defenseless, vulnerable, and open to attack. So, a person whose emotions are of out of control is completely vulnerable for any attack the Devil wants to throw at them. So, when others around us are in a rage and drama is the flavor of the day, it is all the more critical that somebody keeps his or her cool—someone like an Abigail.

Are you an Abigail, or are you the person that others keep telling to calm down because your emotions are out of control? If Abigail allowed her own emotions to take over, then she could not have had the wits about her to stop this oncoming slaughter. This is why doctors, emergency personnel, pilots and soldiers are put through all kinds of hard, emotionally charged and almost impossible situations as they are being trained. You do not want them falling apart in an emergency—lives are at stake. Abigail could not afford to fall to pieces; too much was on the line.

She met the immediate need. She knew just what to do, and she went into action. Did you see the meal she assembled in a matter of moments? Remember that her husband ran a huge business, and they had a large household with many servants. Their pantry would make any food lover's mouth water. It was also a feast day, so naturally a lot of food would have already been prepared. Look at 1 Samuel 25:18 at the supplies she gathers right away to take to David and his men.

David was hungry and tired. His men were hungry and tired. It was a feast day, a time for rest, refreshment, and rejoicing. They had worked hard to protect Nabal's shepherds and all they wanted was a little respect and some food to go with it. Do not overlook the fact that Abigail met the immediate need and request. She did not just go out and try to reason with them without taking care of the first problem.

This might seem like a silly example but think about it this way. If you have children, and your little child is having a nuclear meltdown temper tantrum, you could face the tantrum head on and punish him or her for throwing a fit. But you would be wise to consider "why" he or she is behaving that way. Maybe he is really hungry, needs a nap or both. I'm not saying ignore the temper, but maybe if you get the child some nutritious food and a nap you would see a difference. I am not saying that you bribe the child to get them to calm down, but if they are over-tired and lacking food, they will not be very reasonable. That takes a cool head and discernment to know what the child needs at the time. If the parent just loses his or her temper, then we merely join in with the kids' drama and they will not be taught how to properly handle their own emotions. Seek, like Abigail, to discern what the immediate need or concern is.

Another example is found in Acts 6. The brethren were murmuring against each other because certain Greek widows were being neglected in the daily care that was given to Jewish widows. It was a recipe for a big emotionally charged fight based on ethnic differences (Greeks versus Jews). The apostles dealt with the immediate need: they appointed seven men to make sure the Greek widows had the provisions they needed. The apostles could have spent time teaching, exhorting, and rebuking about proper attitudes toward brethren of all backgrounds, but the Greek widows would still be hungry. They dealt with the immediate need.

Abigail knew the way to a man's heart, and she took care of the issue at hand first before she began to attempt to reason with David. When tempers are soaring high, we have to look past all of that and see what the need is that is not being met, and maybe meeting that need will help diffuse some of the current tension.

She did not make excuses for Nabal's behavior. I have heard Abigail called an "enabler" because of how she tried to take the blame for Nabal. Abigail was not in any way enabling Nabal's behavior. There was nothing in her power to improve or change Nabal. He was not changing for anyone, period, no matter what Abigail said or did. When she came before David, she said openly that her husband lives up to his name, "fool." Her husband's bad character was a reality that was well known to everyone, and she merely acknowledged it. Sometimes a spouse or friend will think he is doing a loved one a favor by making excuses for bad behavior or try to cover it up, but it will only make matters far worse. Abigail was not trying to cover up Nabal's wicked ways, she is trying to save a lot of people from being slaughtered, and she calls her husband out for what he is in order to show that this was his decision, not hers, to treat David and his men that way.

A wise elderly sister once told me that you have to deal with what is, not with what should be. Abigail deserved a better husband than this. David deserved better treatment than this. Nabal should never have talked or behaved in such an evil way, but he did, and that's where Abigail found herself, in the wake of her husband's bad deeds once again. How many times has a wife found herself drowning in the consequences of her husband's lack of character? What is she to do?

Was she a submissive wife? She called her husband a fool. She went behind his back and without his blessing. Twice in this account she withheld information from her husband (1 Samuel 25:19, 36). She knew it would do no good to tell him certain things. However, that does not make her "un-submissive" as a wife.

The apostles said, "We ought to obey God rather than man" Acts 5:29, so there are times when it is impossible to obey man and still be pleasing to God. What if a spouse wants you to stay home from church? Do I please my spouse or obey Jesus? There should never be a conflict in that area, but sadly in too many relationships, there is. "Wives [are to] submit to [their] husbands, as to the Lord." Ephesians 5:22 Their submission is first and foremost to Jesus, so if there is a conflict, the wife has to obey Jesus. I have known of several women who had to "sneak" their giving to the Lord because their husbands did not want money going to God or to a needy person.

What if you are in a car in the passenger seat and the driver is falling asleep? Do you remain silent, or do you reach over and grab the steering wheel to keep from going into the ditch? You take hold of the wheel, because although you are in the passenger seat, you do not feel like dying that night.

Abigail is a submissive wife who loves God and is trying to make the best of the situation she has been given. I am not writing this to justify throwing off respect for authority and to ease our conscience for not obeying those over us just because we don't agree with others' rules or leadership styles. God knows your heart, and if you are seeking to ignore authority to do things your way, He knows. That is not the spirit of Abigail displayed here.

She appealed to David with calm, godly reasoning. Notice that although she could not talk to Nabal this way, she firmly believed she could approach David with a spiritual line of reasoning. Her husband was unreasonable, unspiritual, and unapproachable. Not David, though, even though he has snapped and is on a rampage. She still believed that she could talk some sense into David.

Here are a few of the points Abigail made to David:

- David, God is working in your life, and He fights for you, and all your enemies (Saul, Nabal, etc.) will be punished by God. You have no need to take vengeance into your own hands. God is looking out for you. (See 1 Samuel 25:29)
- David, think of the consequences of your actions. When you become king, do you want this deed hanging over you? Do you really want to be remembered this way? (See 1 Samuel 25:30a)
- David, when you are made king, remember me. (See 1 Samuel 25:31b)

Because of the words of Abigail, because of her wisdom in how to properly handle a volatile situation, many people were spared that day. David proved himself to be a great and humble man, because unlike Nabal, he listened to Abigail. Even though he had vowed to his men to destroy Nabal's household, he backed down and calmed his temper. It can all be credited to a woman like Abigail who had discretion. It made all the difference.

In the end, Nabal is struck by the Lord with a heart disease and dies. Abigail is then brought into David's house to be his wife.

I know a lot of women like Abigail. Women whose husbands are not walking with Jesus, but they continue faithfully teaching their children and leading them to Jesus. God bless you richly for this. I also know women who helped calm down situations and have kept good men from walking off the cliff of bad decisions. God bless you dear sisters for being an Abigail.

Abigail was in a troubled marriage with a very difficult man. She also faced a crisis situation where she could have lost the whole household because of her husband's arrogance and David's anger. But see this woman. See what Abigail did with the wisdom God gave her.

—*Lesson 8 Discussion*—

1. When a godly woman is married to a destructive and unapproachable husband, what are some of the problems that may arise in the home?

2. How does a godly wife balance submission to the husband (and respect for him) while at the same time doing the right thing and submitting to God?

Lesson 9
Seeing a Woman
Work Alongside Her Husband

Priscilla (or Prisca), wife of Aquila—Acts 18

WIFE. TENTMAKER. HOSPITABLE HOST. Missionary. Teacher. Servant of
Jesus Christ.

If you are married, do you consider yourself to be a partner with your
husband in the service of Jesus? Are you and your spouse working together
as a unit, one flesh joined together in the same mind and purpose? Or are
you working as two Christians who just so happen to be married? Do you
see that there is a significant difference between serving Jesus as individuals
and working as one flesh with your spouse?

In this chapter, we will consider another woman mentioned in Scripture who
devoted her life to God, but we will not do so this time without continually
mentioning her husband who is always mentioned with her. Priscilla and
Aquila were truly one flesh, in every sense of the word.

Acts 18:1–3 says, "After these things Paul…went to Corinth. And he found
a certain Jew named Aquila, born in Pontus, who had recently come from
Italy with his wife Priscilla (because Claudius had commanded all the Jews
to depart from Rome); and he came to them. So, because he was of the
same trade, he stayed with them and worked; for by occupation, they were
tentmakers."

Jewish tentmakers who became Christians.

Paul, in his second missionary journey, came from Athens to the very
vibrant, yet wicked, port city of Corinth. As we just read in Acts 18:1–3,
Aquila and Priscilla were tentmakers of Jewish heritage. They were forced
from their homes and had to leave Italy, because the Roman Emperor,
Claudius, kicked all the Jews out of Rome in roughly AD 49. Claudius
was the Roman emperor who reigned from 41 until his death in 54. His

command for Jews to leave Rome was also recorded by the Roman historian Suetonius who wrote that Claudius expelled the Jews from Rome, who were constantly exciting tumults under their leader, Chrestus. Some commentators suggest that this "Chrestus" was Jesus Christ, and that the troubles and violent uproars that were being caused were a result of the Jews trying to stop the spread of Christianity.

Priscilla and Aquila were uprooted from their home in Italy and ended up in Corinth, which was some 600 miles from Rome as the crow flies. Why Corinth? I do not know, except for the providential guidance of God. Maybe business was good for tentmaking in Corinth. Regardless, Paul, as a fellow tentmaker, went to work with them in two trades: tentmaking and disciple-making.

Was it at this time that Priscilla and Aquila became Christians, or were they already Christians long before meeting Paul? We do not know, but we do know what inspired writers like Paul and Luke to write about them and their character.

> Greet Priscilla and Aquila, my fellow workers in Christ Jesus, who risked their own necks for my life, to whom not only I give thanks, but also all the churches of the Gentiles. Likewise greet the church that is in their house.
> (Romans 16:3–5)

Wow. What a wonderful greeting from the heart and soul of one of the most devoted followers and selfless servants of Christ to ever walk the planet—the apostle Paul. Look again at the above passage. Meditate on it.

My fellow workers in Christ Jesus.

Paul used the word *sunergos,* which simply means to work together. This word is the basis for our English word synergy, which means "the interaction of two or more agents or forces so that their combined effect is greater than the sum of their individual effects" (*thefreedictionary.com*). Many good brothers and sisters in Christ were called fellow workers by Paul—Paul did not spread the gospel to the whole world by himself. There were many selfless servants of Jesus Christ who risked their necks, sacrificed their lives and material goods, and devoted themselves to the high purpose and calling of reaching lost souls with the good news of Jesus. Synergy. Many souls joined their energy, resources, and talents together so that through their cooperation, the combined efforts resulted in a greater harvest of souls. "Each part doing its share." (Ephesians 4:16)

Priscilla was truly "one flesh" with Aquila. They were not simply individual Christians who just so happened to be married. They were "one flesh" in every sense of the term. You do not see one without the other. They worked together. They were hospitable together. They traveled together. They taught together. They risked their necks together. Priscilla and Aquila were a team, joined together in one common purpose, to serve the Lord Jesus Christ and His people in whatever way He saw fit.

Synergy was also demonstrated in this godly marriage. Their combined efforts resulted in a greater good than if they were to work as individuals doing "their own thing" for Jesus. Sometimes husbands and wives attempt to work in the kingdom and serve Jesus, but they do so as individuals and not as a unit ("one flesh"). Maybe it is because the husband or wife does not value the other's talents and unique perspectives. Maybe it is a power struggle going on within the marriage. Maybe it is just pure selfishness and pride masked with a label called "my ministry." Each spouse just goes his or her own way, even though they claim to serve the same Lord and serve the same church.

This does not mean that all couples in Christ must have the same gifts and talents or work in the same trade as Priscilla and Aquila. We are, however, called by God to be "one flesh" and that must by definition include our labor in the kingdom of heaven. Think about it, why do shepherds and deacons in God's churches have to be married (see 1 Timothy 3)? There must be something to God's design in two souls united together in Christ with one common purpose and mission.

This is not to say that single people cannot effectively serve God. That is not the point. What is the point is that if two Christians are married, then they must truly sit down and prayerfully consider whether they are serving Christ as a couple or as two Christians who happen to share the same address.

They risked their necks for Paul's life.

As we read, they ministered in the gospel with Paul in Corinth. The hardship that Paul faced in Corinth was to the degree that the Lord directly comforted Paul with His own voice (Acts 18:9–10). Take note Priscilla and Aquila were right there with him. They are risking their safety and lives, too!

When Paul moved on to Ephesus, they traveled with him and continued alongside Paul preaching the gospel to lost souls and encouraging the new brethren in Christ (Acts 18:18–20). In fact, Paul left them in Ephesus while he went to Caesarea and to Antioch (Acts 18:19–22). Ephesus was described by Paul as a place with many open doors for the gospel, but also filled with many adversaries (1 Corinthians 16:8–9). Ephesus was a really tough place for a Christian to be, for example consider the riot that occurred in Acts 19 because of the truth of Christ. The young minister Timothy faced great hardship while in Ephesus, and apparently so did Priscilla and Aquila, a couple who "risked their necks for Paul's life." They did it for the Lord, yes, but they also did it for Paul.

Are there people in your life that have taken great risks and personal sacrifice to serve you? Have you done that for others? Think of the excuses and cop-outs Priscilla and Aquila could have made to back out of the opportunities given them to serve Christ and His body. Too dangerous. Too far from home. Too busy. Too much to ask of us.

The church that is in their house.

Priscilla and Aquila served as host to local congregations of Christians in the various cities in which they lived. On more than one occasion and in more than one city, the local church assembled and worshiped in the home of Priscilla and Aquila. When they traveled from Corinth to Ephesus with Paul, they opened their home to the church. Paul wrote 1 Corinthians when he was in Ephesus with Priscilla and Aquila (1 Corinthians 16:19). At some point, Priscilla and Aquila moved back to Rome, because when Paul wrote to the brethren in Rome, he greeted Priscilla and Aquila and the church that met in their house (Romans 16:3–5). Not only did they host the worship assemblies of the local congregations, they also housed Paul in Corinth when they first met him. He was welcomed into their home, and he stayed with them (Acts 18:3).

There is a considerable amount of sacrifice to set time, plans, resources, and personal space aside to be host to others. There is a reason why Peter said to show hospitality without grumbling (1 Peter 4:10). Giving and sharing can take a toll on you, but we are encouraged by the Hebrew writer to "not forget to do good and to share, for with such sacrifices God is well pleased" (Hebrews 13:16). It is important for us to keep in mind that our sacrifices for others should first and foremost be because of our love for Jesus and out of gratitude for His ultimate sacrifice for us on the cross. We look to minister to others because Jesus continually ministers to us. Our riches are His riches. Our time is His time. Our lives are His lives. Our homes are His homes. Our glory is His glory. For us to share our time, energy and things with others is a very small thing in comparison to what Jesus has done, always does and will forever do for us. I believe Priscilla and Aquila understood this and lived it.

They took Apollos aside.

While ministering in Ephesus, Priscilla and Aquila came to the synagogue and heard a powerful speaker named Apollos teaching about Jesus. He was well-educated and came from Alexandria which was a renowned center of education. He taught truth, but not the whole truth. So, they lovingly took Apollos aside to explain to him the way of the Lord more accurately. Their goal was to show Apollos the complete teaching about Jesus, to refine him, and to help him mature in the doctrine.

> Now a certain Jew named Apollos, born at Alexandria, an eloquent man and mighty in the Scriptures, came to Ephesus. This man had been instructed in the way of the Lord; and being fervent in spirit, he spoke and taught accurately the things of the Lord, though he knew only the baptism of John. So, he began to speak boldly in the synagogue. When Aquila and Priscilla heard him, they took him aside and explained to him the way of God more accurately. And when he desired to cross to Achaia, the brethren wrote, exhorting the disciples to receive him; and when he arrived, he greatly helped those who had believed through grace; for he vigorously refuted the

Jews publicly, showing from the Scriptures that Jesus is the Christ (Acts 18:24–28).

Sometimes we will encounter a Christian who needs some teaching and guidance, and we delay and avoid our duty to help guide him to a better understanding. Or we talk to others about how that person needs to grow and change. Or maybe we just say, "Bless her heart, she'll figure it out in time." Therefore, that person is stunted in his or her growth because of our negligence.

Other times we see another who needs to grow, and we approach it in the wrong way, so the one who should have been encouraged and uplifted by us ends up walking away feeling brow-beaten and demoralized. Priscilla and Aquila loved Apollos enough to train him, but they did it in a way that was helpful.

Because of the kind teaching and efforts of Priscilla along with her husband Aquila, Apollos became a powerful force in the kingdom. When he desired to travel on to the region of Achaia, he was encouraged by the brothers (including no doubt Priscilla and Aquila). When he arrived in Achaia, "he greatly helped those who had believed through grace; for he vigorously refuted the Jews publicly, showing from the Scriptures that Jesus is the Christ" (Acts 18:27b–28). See what a tremendous effect this godly couple had upon Apollos and therefore by extension upon many more people! Apollos was described as the one who watered the gospel seed that Paul sowed (1 Corinthians 3:6). Seed does not grow without water, and the souls who were taught by Paul were later encouraged by Apollos. Who set Apollos on solid ground so that he could be that watering can for Jesus? Priscilla and Aquila!

Greet Priscilla and Aquila.

Paul loved them dearly, and so did the brethren throughout the Gentile world. Paul as well as many Gentile Christians owed them a tremendous debt of gratitude as Paul noted in Romans 16:3–5. I am sure that Priscilla and Aquila did not see things the same way. They clearly do not seem to be the types who were out for glory, praise, and attention, they were simply servants who loved God, loved each other, and loved the brethren.

In Paul's final letter, as he is about to be beheaded for the cause of Christ, he sends out one final greeting to Priscilla (Prisca) and Aquila as we find them back again in Asia, this time in some close proximity to Timothy (2 Timothy 4:19). We do not know where Priscilla and Aquila ended up, or what happened to them after Paul died. We do know however that they left for us an incredible testimony to the power of a Christian couple joined together in the same mind and purpose.

—Lesson 9 Discussion—

1. What are some ways you and your spouse can be the Priscilla's and Aquila's in the church?

2. Who is the Apollos around you that you can encourage, instruct, and mentor?

3. Who is the Paul around you that you can work alongside in the Lord?

Lesson 10
Seeing Women Who Needed to Get Along

Euodia and Syntyche—Philippians 4:1–4

A LONG-AWAITED LETTER.

Picture yourself back in New Testament times when the congregation in Philippi received a letter from the beloved apostle Paul as he sat in a Roman prison. As the congregation assembled together, they are filled with excitement and great anticipation as the letter is read publicly. This is every saint's first time to hear Paul's special words from God for them. They did not have a copy machine, so this was the only copy available for the whole church until someone could hand copy the letter. Today we can freely and quickly send information to outer space and back, and we can turn on our smartphones or tablets and have a live video conversation with someone thousands of miles away. We can see them, and they can see us in real time. It seems to be no big deal anymore for most in Western Civilization to communicate across the globe; in fact, most of us probably take it for granted.

We may not be able to grasp how incredibly valuable this letter from Paul was that traveled by land and sea from Rome to Philippi. They had been waiting for news and encouragement from the man who is responsible for their beginnings in Jesus Christ (see Acts 16).

Philippians 2 indicates that it was Epaphroditus that hand-delivered this letter to the brethren. He was the messenger that the brethren at Philippi had sent to Paul to bring things to aid Paul with his necessities. We also know from Philippians 2 that the brethren heard that Epaphroditus was sick and almost died, and they were greatly concerned about his welfare. Paul sent this letter in the hands of Epaphroditus as a way to comfort and encourage the brethren even more.

These Christians at Philippi, "from the very first day" of their salvation, supported Paul's ministry in multiple ways, especially by sending him funds "once and again" as he was in other locations preaching the gospel (Philippians 1:5; 4:16). They were hard-working, loving, dedicated servants of Jesus. Paul loved them dearly (Philippians 1:3–9).

A letter all about the mindset of Jesus Christ.

So now the church is assembled, and the letter is read. Paul's short letter is jam-packed with teaching and examples concerning having the mindset of Jesus Christ. Paul had that focus (Philippians 1 and 3). Timothy and Epaphroditus had that focus (Philippians 2). Jesus demonstrated the ultimate example of that mindset by leaving heaven and coming down to die on the cross (Philippians 2). Some did not have this focus and they became enemies of the cross of Christ, and it made Paul weep (Philippians 3).

As they near the conclusion of the letter, Paul singled out two women in the church at Philippi for a special exhortation about their own mindset and he also addressed the congregation about their responsibility toward these two sisters. Let us consider what these sisters heard from Paul as this letter was read in front of the whole congregation.

> Therefore, my beloved and longed-for brethren, my joy and crown, so stand fast in the Lord, beloved. I implore Euodia and I implore Syntyche to be of the same mind in the Lord. And I urge you also, true companion, help these women who labored with me in the gospel, with Clement also, and the rest of my fellow workers, whose names are in the Book of Life. Rejoice in the Lord always. Again I will say, rejoice! (Philippians 4:1–4)

Are your ears burning?

Can you imagine sitting in the assembly and hearing your name singled out by the apostle Paul in this letter? Even more, can you picture sitting there as Paul in his letter tells you and the other sister to get along in the Lord? How did he know? Would your face turn red? How would you respond to being singled out for this exhortation by God's apostle?

I'm begging you!

Paul used this verb "implore" twice, once for each woman. The word is *parakaloo,* which means to call near to one's side; it is also translated "urge", "plead", "beseech", "entreat." I like the word "beg." I beg Euodia…I beg Syntyche. Whatever was going on between Euodia and Syntyche is unknown to us, but just like the situations in the church at Corinth (1 Corinthians 1:11; 11:18) it was a matter that had come to Paul's attention and required his Spirit-led input to guide them.

The issue is never really the issue.

Christians get bent out of shape over something and think that some issue, decision, or course of action is worth the fight. Because of that determination to win or to prove ourselves justified, we end up severing relationships, hurting feelings, and slowing down the work that we should be accomplishing for Jesus. The issue or decision that was supposed to be the thing we were discussing was forgotten long ago, and it becomes about personalities, long-held resentment, and bitterness, who is more involved in the church, who has been here longer, who knows more, etc.

Did you notice in the text that Paul never addressed the specific issues between Euodia and Syntyche? He didn't say, "Euodia, you were right on this topic concerning helping the widows." Or "Syntyche, your way of doing things is better suited for teaching the young women than the way sister Euodia really wants to do it." No, because the issue was not the real problem. What really mattered was that Paul begged them to keep working for the Lord, but to do it joined together in unison.

Synergy.

We discussed this word in the previous chapter about Priscilla and Aquila. Once again, the word *sunergos* (translated fellow workers in Philippians 4:3) is used by Paul in reference to Euodia, Syntyche and many others. These ladies were strong-minded workers determined to work as hard as they could for Jesus and for Paul. They are going to heaven—their names are in the Book of Life. Paul tells the congregation to assist these two sisters in their work. It tells you a lot about these two women, doesn't it? They wanted to do great things for Jesus, and they were working tirelessly in their work. However, Paul is telling them that doing great things for Jesus is not enough. They must be united as a team, joined together with one mind, as they served the Lord Jesus.

In the same way we considered Priscilla and Aquila's "synergy" for Jesus, we must also consider the way brothers and sisters work for Jesus. Way too often we work as individuals doing our own thing, going our own way, focused on our "ministry," but we are not together in spirit. As long as I work on my task for the Lord and you work on yours, we do just fine, but what happens when we cross paths? When you and I are working on the same task, then your strong opinions cross my strong opinions, and then what? What happens when you don't teach a class the way I think you should? What happens when we don't agree on which Bible curriculum we should use for the kids' classes? How do we handle our disagreements on how to raise our kids, how to educate and discipline them? We both have ideas for how the classrooms should be decorated and furnished, now what?

When we worked independently and left each other alone, everything was great, right? Wrong! It was not okay, because Christ did not save us and leave us to be individuals operating independently. He placed us within a body, both in a universal and a local sense. All Christians everywhere in the world are part of one body of which Christ is the head (Ephesians 1:21–22), but Christians are to work together locally with Christians, assembling as one body and one family to worship, to build each other up, to reach out to save souls, etc. Paul tells the local body of believers in Philippi to be of the same mind, just like a body with hands, feet, eyes, and ears working for the same purpose (1 Corinthians 12:11–27). Euodia and Syntyche were not doing that, even though as individuals they were doing good works for the Lord. A pile of body parts doesn't make a body.

Paul doesn't have to correct their servant attitude, he doesn't have to tell them to get busy for Jesus, but he has to exhort them apparently to stop butting heads, forsake the opinionated junk, and work together for Jesus as a unit. We must be reminded of the words of God through Amos when He asked, "Can two walk together unless they are agreed?" (Amos 3:3)

When you have two very strong people with strong minds and strong wills laboring for God, they sometimes will lock horns because of various differences. As that happens, everyone else is affected because we are a body and family, and the true work of God is side-tracked. However, when those strong-minded brothers and sisters put aside their differences and humble themselves and submit their minds to the real work of Christ, it is a powerful and unstoppable force for good. The church at Philippi was doing great things for Jesus and Paul, but they will be even greater when they work as one mind, in harmony of spirit.

Help these women who labored with me in the gospel.

Euodia and Syntyche were women of the best intentions, and they had servant hearts. The church at Philippi began with strong women (Acts 16:11–15). Of course, by the time of the writing of this epistle, Philippi had elders and deacons, but they still had strong women. These women aren't to just fade away into inactivity because they now had elders and deacons. Paul tells the congregation to help these women in their work as they are fellowshipping in the gospel. Whatever these two sisters were doing, whatever work they were involved in, Paul tells the brothers and sisters to be an encouragement and support to them in their work for Christ.

The kingdom needs strong-minded, servant-hearted women. Strong-minded is not to be confused with giving people a piece of your mind, nor does it mean being stubborn and unwilling to consider other viewpoints. This balance comes when we become "one mind" in Jesus. Our strengths, our talents are tempered and guided by the love and humility of Jesus.

God's work, not mine.

Paul's letter to the Philippians often mentioned joy and rejoicing, but that is not what the letter to the Philippians is primarily about. He often used words like "mindset" and "mind" in this letter, but Paul was trying to get at more than the power of positive thinking.

If you go through this short letter, and underline or highlight all the times Paul says Lord, God, Jesus, Christ, or Savior then you will begin to understand the theme of Philippians. Why did Paul endure such cruel suffering and harsh treatment? Because it is all about Jesus (Philippians 1:21, 29–30; 3:10). Why did Jesus leave heaven's glory to die on the cross? Because it was God's work and God's glory that would be accomplished (Philippians 2:4–11). Why did Timothy put his own interests aside and sincerely care for the brethren? Because Timothy sought the things of the Lord Jesus, not his own things (Philippians 2:19–21). Why did Epaphroditus come close to death? Because he did everything "for the work of Christ… not regarding his own life." Philippians 2:30 Why did Paul want to stay on earth and help Christians when he would much rather die and be with Jesus? Because he was all about serving Jesus and doing His work for His people (Philippians 1:19–26).

It is God's work that He begun in the Philippian disciples, and it is God that continued to work in them and through them (Philippians 1:6; 2:13). Paul considered himself just an instrument in the hands of the Great Physician. Euodia and Syntyche needed to be reminded of this valuable principle. It is not our ministry. It is not our church. It is not our money. They are not our Bible classes. It is not our worship service. Those people being taught are not our people. It's all about Jesus. It is His work. "For we are His workmanship, created in Christ Jesus for good works." (Ephesians 2:10)

My mother shared with me some very simple yet powerful words as I began my first full-time preaching position in Columbus, Ohio. She said with tear-dimmed eyes, "Remember who your Master is." How right she was. Once we fully grasp that, and once we as individual Christians own that concept, then we can begin to view ourselves as merely instruments and servants of the Master. We see the value in others walking along with us as partners, sharing in the work together, side by side. We stop looking for ways to get the credit for teaching someone or having the best ideas, and we look to lift up other brethren and point out their great worth and their ways of contributing to the family and body of Christ. We will listen to other ideas and consider other ways of doing things instead of saying, "This is the way we've always done such and such."

Being of one mind.

This means we are focused on the same purpose. We have the same Lord. We are on the same team. We believe in the same goal and have the same purpose. We have the same enemy and we are on the same side in the conflict against the Devil. Look for the word "same" in the letter to the Philippians—it is very instructive.

This requires listening to each other. This requires valuing other's input. This requires stopping to consider the feelings of others. We have to take the foot off the accelerator sometimes and remember that the task is not as important as our relationships with each other.

If we accomplished the job, but we hurt people and alienated them along the way, then was it worth it? Of course not. If we finished the project but did it alone when it would have been better to join with others, then we missed the greater purpose. If we finished the task, but stepped all over another brother or sister's feelings, then what did we really accomplish? God doesn't want individuals living to themselves. He wants a body. He wants a family.

Let us be of one mind, serving together side by side for Jesus, as Paul encouraged these two sisters in Philippi to remember.

—Lesson 10 Discussion—

1. Are you in a Euodia and Syntyche relationship? Is there strife instead of synergy in your working relationship with your fellow workers in Christ?

2. Why are you and Syntyche not getting along? What's the root cause, and how can you help to address the situation to bring about a unified mindset?

3. How will you help the Euodia's and Syntyche's around you?

Lesson 11
Seeing a Woman
Who Was a Mother in Israel

Deborah the Judge—Judges 4—5

WHAT THOUGHTS COME TO MIND when you say the word, "Mom?" Comfort. Reassurance. Good food. Wise counsel. Safe place. It's who we want to go to when all is falling apart. We want our moms. She is the one we seek out when we are scared. We turn to mom when we don't know what to do or where to go. She is the one upon whom we pour out our souls. Mom is the one who gives us hope. She is the one who directs our hearts to the Lord.

Not everyone has had that blessed experience with their biological mother. But if you look around, I'm sure there is someone else who either has served in that role or will serve in that role for you. The nation of Israel was in a spot where they needed a mother. Notice that they did not turn to their own mothers, but they all looked to Deborah as their mother.

Israel put themselves in a mess.

Israel was in a downward spiral of spiritual degradation. They were a mess. The book of Judges is often accurately summed up by its very last verse, "In those days, there was no king in Israel; everyone did what was right in his own eyes." (Judges 21:25)

The second chapter of Judges also lays out what happened repeatedly to the nation of Israel. Things are going great, folks are following God and there is peace, and then a new generation grows up that does not know God. That new generation begins to learn and follow the ways of the idolatrous and pagan people living among them. Then God's righteous anger burned against them, and He sold them into the hands of their enemies, and they were harshly oppressed. Out of their agony, the people of Israel cry out to God for mercy and deliverance; and God, because He is rich in mercy, answered the call. He sent a judge to deliver them and rescue them from the hands of those who oppressed them. Then the land has rest, and the cycle repeats whenever the judge died.

Over and over the story goes through the book, except that it gets worse as you go—by the end of the book, there are some very dark and disturbing things that are happening. By the end of Judges, there is no rest and peace. So, that is the setting of the life of Deborah. The people of Israel, according to Deborah, "Israel chose new gods, then there was war in the gates." Judges 5:8 Judges 4 begins with, "When Ehud was dead, the children again did evil in the sight of the Lord. So the Lord sold them into the hand of Jabin king of Canaan, who reigned in Hazor." It is interesting to note that in the days of Joshua, Joshua and his army defeated a Jabin king of Hazor and burned the city of Hazor with fire (Joshua 11). Some have suggested that this new Jabin is a descendant of the first one, but regardless, it is a lesson that God's enemies don't stay gone forever. They rebuild and regroup.

Jabin king of Canaan had a massive army that was supported by 900 chariots and the commander of his army was Sisera. The Bible records that they "harshly oppressed" the children of Israel for 20 years (Judges 4:3). 20 years! Deborah pointed out in her song in Judges 5 that before she arose as a mother in Israel, that village life had ceased, and that the highways were deserted because they were no longer safe (Judges 5:6–7). She also recounted that "not a shield or spear was seen among forty thousand in Israel." Judges 5:8 The forces of Jabin and Sisera had successfully disarmed Israel and were terrorizing them without any fear of rebellion. Who could stand up against such an overwhelming force?

The world is a cruel master, and when we leave God, He will give us over to those masters, and it is a world without mercy and hope. The only hope for us is that we see our own wretchedness and turn back to the Lord. Israel, at least some of Israel, was at this point.

Things were bad. They were oppressed, crushed, poorly armed and terrorized. Faithful men were hard to find. It seems from Deborah's words in chapter 5 that many saw a need but did not have the courage to stand up or engage.

God raised up a mother in Israel.

Deborah arose as a mother in Israel when Israel needed someone to turn to.

"And she would sit under the palm tree of Deborah between Ramah and Bethel in the mountains of Ephraim. And the children of Israel came up to her for judgment" (Judges 4:5). You know, someone just does not sit under a palm tree with a sign saying, "I'm God's judge," and people immediately start coming. Judges 2:18 says that "The Lord was with the judge." Somehow it was made plain to the people that God was with Deborah. She was called a "prophetess," so God was making His words known clearly through her (Judges 4:4).

They came to her for judgment, I believe, because they had come to know that God was with her. Where else in Israel would they get a fair shake? Who else would hear their case and give an equitable judgment? Not their oppressors. Not the corrupt priesthood of Israel. By the way, the priests were supposed to be Israel's judges (Leviticus 10:8–11; Ezekiel 44:23–24). Where are they? Why aren't the people of Israel going to them? Considering Israel's religious state, it is safe to assume that the priesthood also had mostly left God. The people of Israel recognized God's presence in Deborah's life, and that she was righteous. She would give fair treatment to all. In the times where everyone did what was right in his own eyes; Israel needed a judge who did not live by that same standard. That judge was Deborah.

Why do people in the world today seek out Christians for relationships and for advice? Do they not, as Israel did with Deborah, see light in the midst of darkness? What do they see in you? Do they see a Deborah? Do they see someone who is full of the Lord's presence?

Deborah arose as a mother in Israel when its leaders needed encouragement and strength to engage the enemy.

Then she sent and called for Barak the son of Abinoam from Kedesh in Naphtali, and said to him, "Has not the Lord God of Israel commanded, 'Go and deploy troops at Mount Tabor; take with you 10,000 men of the sons of Naphtali and of the sons of Zebulun; and against you I will deploy Sisera, the commander of Jabin's army, with his chariots and his multitude at the River Kishon; and I will deliver him to your hand?'" (Judges 4:6–7)

She sent and called him.

Barak was called and commanded by God for a purpose, but someone had to send for him, encourage him, and strengthen him to fulfill that God-given task. She was called to be the prophetess and judge in Israel, Barak was called to be the military leader in this battle. She was not called to do his job, and he was not called to do hers. Each had a responsibility and role. But even though leading the soldiers into battle was not Deborah's calling, she recognized her role was to give courage to the man called to do it. With the command of God came the assurance that God would be with them, and that God would deliver the enemy into Barak's hand. Take notice of how the Lord's hand is evident throughout this battle (4:6, 9, 14–15, 23; 5:4, 13). Deborah was very much aware of God's presence and power, not just for her, but for Barak and for Israel to deliver them from their oppressors.

Barak accepted the call, but he asked Deborah to go with him. He told her, "If you go with me, then I will go; but if you will not go with me, I will not go!" Judges 4:8 She responded by telling Barak that she would go, but he would not get the glory, because the glory would go to a woman. I believe she is referring to Jael, the woman who ended up killing Commander Sisera by driving a tent peg through his temple into the ground (Judges 4:17–22; 5:24–27).

Notice that Barak seemed to be fine with not getting the glory. I do not believe that this is a negative mark on Barak that he wanted Deborah to go with him. Barak stood in faith and answered the call from God through Deborah. He led 10,000 men without swords and shields into battle against a well-armed fighting force with 900 chariots. I'm not sure if they had pitchforks, sticks and shovels, but we know they didn't have swords or shields. This was an enemy that had harshly oppressed them for two decades. He would go, and he would lead these soldiers into war, but he wanted Deborah with him. The men of Zebulun, Naphtali and Issachar rushed at Barak's heels into war jeopardizing their own lives to the point of death.

Please take note that Barak is mentioned in Hebrews 11 along with many other heroes of the Jewish faith. Although it makes me wonder why Deborah did not make it on the list, we know that Deborah stirred Barak on to great things and an unwavering faith.

She also reminded Barak that the Lord has already gone out in battle before Him (Judges 4:14). Yes, the Lord was with Deborah, but not only with Deborah. God would be with Barak and his soldiers as well. Barak and his men rushed into battle, and the Lord defeated Jabin and Sisera's army in a mighty way. The Lord fought for Israel.

Not everyone answered the call of God through Deborah, and this is also important for mothers in Israel to remember. The people of Reuben had "great resolves of heart" and "great searchings of heart." (Judges 5:15–16) They really thought about it but did nothing. They knew God called them to battle, and they knew their brethren were in trouble, but they stayed safely beyond the Jordan. They kept separated and aloof from the problems and battles of their brethren. Others also denied the call. The people of Gilead "stayed" beyond the Jordan, the people of Dan "remained" on their ships, and Asher "continued at the seashore and stayed by his inlets." (Judges 5:15–18) The people of "Meroz" were cursed by Deborah and Barak because they did not come to the help of the Lord (Judges 5:23). Barak and his soldiers were not like that. They had faith in God and knew they were called to fight God's enemies and they rushed into the battle. Deborah was not like that, either. She knew Israel needed a mother, and she "arose." She didn't just think about it, she did it.

> "That the leaders led in Israel, and that the people volunteered,
> bless the Lord!" (Judges 5:2)

Consider the power of your influence and your presence in the life of another. I will always remember a dear elderly sister in Columbus, Ohio who would walk in the church building pulling her oxygen cart and she would greet everyone, especially visitors along the way to her seat. She was in constant pain. Her daughter told me that sometimes she would cry in the pew just because the pain was so intense. But she was there, always there. She was encouraging. She smiled at others. She loved God and she loved

His people. Her presence in that worship assembly meant the world to me. I was stronger because she was there. My attitude was better because she was there. She was a mother in Israel.

Here are some final ideas about how you can be a mother in Israel like Deborah.

Be a mother in Israel for a young mom who needs a friend. She may not tell you she needs a friend, in fact, she may say nothing. Sometimes she may even try to put on a good face and pretend she is fine. But she is not. If you are a mom, you know this more than I ever will. Be attentive. Take that young sister under your wing and be her best friend. Everyone may be trying to give her correction and advice, but not everyone will try to be her friend.

Be a mother in Israel by giving encouragement to a preacher or an elder. Listen to them when they sound frustrated and need an ear. Watch the kids for that young preacher so he can take his wife out for a date night (and if you are able give them a little cash to pay for that dinner and a movie). Ask the preacher or elder how you can help make their work lighter. That preacher may be a Barak who has great faith and is called to go to war against Satan and his forces, but he needs a Deborah in his corner telling him God is with him and that God will fight for him.

Be a mother in Israel for a college student away from home. When I was a student at Purdue, the sisters at the Lafayette Church of Christ were exactly that for me and for hundreds of others over the years. Warm, home-cooked meals and a place to hang out on a Friday night.

Be a mother in Israel for children whose parents are not walking with Christ. You may see these kids come with their grandparents because mom and dad don't want to take them to worship God. Find ways to make those kids feel special, accepted, and appreciated. Maybe you see a family where only one parent brings those kids to Bible study and worship. Pour out all the encouragement you possibly can on that parent and the kids. I know one mother in Israel who prepares Christmas stockings for kids like that. God bless her.

Be a mother in Israel for the single women in the church. They might feel like a 3rd wheel and want to fit in somewhere. I know for me it is very easy to forget about the singles in the church. So many of us are caught up in doing couples' things and family things that we do not pay close enough attention to those who do not have a spouse or kids. Be a mother in Israel to them. Be a friend. It's not that you pity them or feel sorry for them; you want them to know that they are just as special and valued and accepted in the kingdom of God.

Deborah arose as a mother in Israel. Will you arise and be a mother in Israel for others around you?

—*Lesson 11 Discussion*—

1.   Who is the Deborah in your life today?

2.   How can you be a Deborah for God's people?

Lesson 12
Seeing a Woman
Who Gave Her Last Two Coins

The Widow's Two Coins—Mark 12:41–44; Luke 21:1–4

TWO SMALL COINS dropped in the offering box and made very little sound.

But it thundered in heaven.

The disciples of Jesus were looking with awe at impressive temple stones and marveling at the amazing complex built by Herod (Mark 13:1). Jesus, on the other hand, had His divine gaze focused upon one poor widow who had just given her last two coins.

This passage has been used many times as God's people prepare to take a collection for the "Lord's work," and the intent here is not to criticize that. It is beyond impressive that this widow gave so sacrificially. She gave her last two coins, "everything" she had to live on, and she was commended by Jesus for doing so. No doubt, this is a great Scripture for encouraging sacrificial giving.

But we need to dive deeper into this passage and to the Scripture as a whole to get a fuller perspective of this text. We will see this woman's condition and the spiritual condition of the Jews in her day with more depth. Once we do this, it will really make what this woman did so amazing! It will leave no doubt as to why this selfless act of sacrificial faith by this widow attracted divine praise.

The Widow's Reality: Loneliness, affliction, poverty and injustice. (James 1:27)

Her husband is dead and gone. She is lonely. Her lifelong companion, the one with whom she shared everything in this world, and the one who most likely provided for her is now no more on this earth. As the old hymn goes, "Be with me Lord, when loneliness overtakes me, when I must weep amidst the fires of pain." Those of us who haven't faced widowhood can't possibly understand the affliction and loneliness of this woman deprived of her spouse.

It is amazing that this poor widow gave all in spite of her profound loneliness and affliction. We can certainly understand that she was lonely and afflicted in being a widow, even if we cannot personally appreciate her pain.

But wait, there's more.

We need to ask some questions here, like, why was this woman so destitute in the first place? What conditions existed in Israel that led to this woman's great poverty? How did she only have two coins left? Where are her kids? Are they poor too? Are they dead? Did she even have kids? Or are they neglecting their mother? We don't have any answers about her kids, but we do have answers from Scripture that speak to this woman's current financial state.

God's heart always went out to the stranger, fatherless, widow and poor (Psalm 68:5; Proverbs 15:25; Jeremiah 49:11). In fact, God on more than one occasion told us His standard of pure religion is founded squarely upon how we treat the powerless and helpless (James 1:27). Our Lord throughout the Bible tells His people to care for the helpless, defend the powerless, and rebuke those who oppressed the afflicted (Isaiah 1:17; Zechariah 7:10). To care for the "least" of Jesus' brethren was equivalent to doing it for Jesus (Matthew 25:31–46). Giving to God, by definition, includes giving to others.

Contained in Moses' law were explicit instructions and direct commands for the people of Israel on how to care for widows (and anyone in a condition of poverty for that matter). Every three years, the Jews were to come and heap up their tithes of produce in their towns, so that the Levites (religious workers) and all the poor could eat and be satisfied (Deuteronomy 14:28–29). They were not to take a widow's garment in a pledge, and they were to farm in such a way as to leave plenty of food for the poor, including widows (Deuteronomy 24:17–22). God had laws for protecting widow's property (Deuteronomy 25:5–10). The people were even to pronounce God's curses upon those who pervert justice due to the helpless and powerless, including the widow (Deuteronomy 27:19).

Included in those instructions is this amazing passage in Deuteronomy 15. I want you to notice this:

- But there will be no poor among you; for the LORD will bless you in the land that the LORD your God is giving you for an inheritance to possess. (v. 4)
- For there will never cease to be poor in the land. Therefore I command you, "You shall open wide your hand to your brother, to the needy and to the poor, in your land." (v. 11)

God through Moses said, "there will be no poor among you," and then turned around in seeming contradiction to say, "for there will never cease to be poor in the land." Which is it, Moses? That's why we need to read Deuteronomy 15:5—"If only you will strictly obey the voice of the LORD your God, being careful to do all this commandment that I command you today."

If only you will strictly obey the voice of the Lord your God.

So, why were there poor in the land in the days of Moses? Because God's people did not obey God's commands to help the poor. That's what God *just said!* So, why did Jesus say that the poor will always be with us (John 12:8)? Is it because He was seeking to excuse us from caring for the poor? Absolutely not, that was the furthest thing from His mind. If you doubt it, go back and re-read everything God (Jesus) wrote in the Law of Moses about caring for the poor.

The reason the poor widow was poor was because God's people around her were not obeying the Law of Moses that Jesus wrote. Our abundance and our riches that God has poured out upon us do not always make it to those who need it the most.

Where there should have been a safety net, instead there was a giant pit where the most helpless fell with no way out. Take note of the text of Mark

12 and Luke 21. How were the rich Jews giving? Out of their abundance! How much where they giving to the temple? Large sums of money!

What God is shouting from the Law of Moses to them is, turn around and see this daughter of Abraham! Stop trying to impress Me by sounding your trumpets with all this cash and step over there and help her!

Let's go further. Look at both Mark and Luke's account of the poor widow. In BOTH accounts, right before the widow gives her last two coins, Jesus condemns the religious leadership for what?

Devouring widow's houses!

> And in his teaching he said, "Beware of the scribes, who…devour widows' houses and for a pretense make long prayers. They will receive the greater condemnation." (Mark 12:38–40; cp. Luke 20:45–47)

The Holy Spirit laid out these documents. Right after talking about the Jewish leadership gobbling up widow's houses (property, money, etc.), the Lord saw fit to highlight this amazing widow's sacrificial gift.

Just before this Jesus cleansed the temple and condemned the Jewish leadership for making God's house into a den of thieves (Luke 19:45–48). They only cared about a widow enough to use her as an illustration to trap Jesus in an argument about the resurrection (Luke 20:27–32). When I go back and read Luke 18 and Jesus' parable about the widow who had to cry out persistently for justice from a wicked judge, it doesn't seem so far-fetched considering the context. Matthew 15 and Mark 7 recount Jesus condemning the Pharisees for not taking care of their parents by conveniently excusing themselves saying they had given that money to God. The Pharisees were clearly lovers of money (Luke 16:14–15).

There was no justice in the land of Israel, and God's people and God's leaders were to blame. The Lord spoke plainly to Israel in the Law about what He would do to them if they perverted justice by not caring for the stranger, fatherless, widow and poor.

You shall not mistreat any widow or fatherless child. If you do mistreat them, and they cry out to me, I will surely hear their cry, and my wrath will burn, and I will kill you with the sword, and your wives shall become widows and your children fatherless. (Exodus 22:22–24)

"Then I will draw near to you for judgment. I will be a swift witness against the sorcerers, against the adulterers, against those who swear falsely, against those who oppress the hired worker in his wages, the widow and the fatherless, against those who thrust aside the sojourner, and do not fear me," says the Lord of hosts. (Malachi 3:5)

Is it any surprise that in both Mark and Luke's accounts that the Holy Spirit transitions to a discussion on the destruction of Jerusalem? It wasn't just the rejection of Jesus by the people of Jerusalem that led to its destruction. God promised swift and severe punishment upon Israel if they behaved this way toward the widows and poor.

Why did the widow only have two coins left? The immediate context of Luke and Mark along with the clear commands in Moses' law answer that question.

The Widow's Heart

This leads us back to the widow and her incredible heart for God.

Her world was not as she desired it. The widow's world in many ways was not as it should have been. Life was kicking her in the teeth, stabbing her in the back, breaking her heart and punching her in the gut. And her own Jewish brethren could have come to her aid, but instead they took whatever she had left and added it to their abundance.

How could she have responded to all of this? She could have just given in to bitterness and resentment for sure. "If this is what it means to be a follower of God, then forget it!" Or "The people down at the temple have enough of my money!" Or "My two little coins won't make a difference anyways!"

But she gave all she could for her God. "All she had to live on."
(Mark 12:44b)

According to Olive Tree Bible, these two coins (*lepta*) make a *kodrantes*. A *kodrantes* (Latin *quadrans*) was a Roman copper coin worth about 1/64 of a denarius, which was a day's wage for a laborer (Mark 12:42). All this woman had left was 1/64 of a day's wage.

It is evident to me that this poor widow saw all of her money and all of her being as belonging to the Lord. Many times, we give thinking what we put in the collection basket is the Lord's money, and the rest is ours. Wrong! It's all the Lord's money!

The book of Luke has as bookends two widows at the temple that gave all for their God. Anna the prophetess (Luke 2:36–38) and this poor widow who gave all (Luke 21). What a testimony to the heart of the outcast and rejected who out of faith for God and love for Him give all they can.

The Widow's Lord

We've looked at the widow's reality, and then marveled at her amazing heart in the midst of such pain, poverty and injustice. Now let's talk about her Lord.

Observe that in these texts, Jesus sat "opposite" the treasury. He placed Himself there to watch "how" people gave (Mark 12:41). This same place, the treasury, is where widows were robbed. This treasury had become a den of thieves. This same place is where they had previously tried to stone Jesus after He called them the devil's children while at the same time called Himself the I AM (John 8:20). It is so ironic that the Jewish leadership refused to put Jesus' blood money in the treasury when Judas tried to return it (Matthew 27:6).

The treasury in the temple was the symbol of corruption, oppression, hypocrisy, and murder. Jesus adds to this in Matthew 6:2 when He addressed how the hypocrites sounded the trumpets when they gave. Alfred Edersheim in his work on the Jewish Temple wrote that there were trumpet-shaped offering boxes in the treasury. It may be that Jesus was playing off of this imagery when He spoke of the hypocrites sounding their trumpets. You can imagine there was a lot of noise being made when the rich put large sums of money in these collection trumpets.

As I wrote at the beginning, there was very little sound made when this poor widow dropped in those two small coins. No one noticed. Except for the Lord of heaven and earth. Like so many times in His ministry, Jesus called His disciples to *see* what they were not seeing. Clearly the disciples didn't notice it, because Jesus had to point it out to them.

Jesus called his disciples to him and said to them (Mark 12:43).

This widow's Lord noticed, even if no one else did. The God who created this woman would richly bless her for her faith and sacrifice, even if she never had another penny to her name. These are the people Jesus said would come and sit down in the kingdom of heaven.

Here are a few more things to take to heart:

- Injustice exists. You and I live in a world of things that should not be. But Jesus will deal with injustice one day. Our response is to live for Jesus and give our all for Him, whatever our "all" is.
- Jesus sees us in our "religion." He sees if we are like those who are giving because it's easy, convenient and makes us look good. He sees if we are giving like this widow with a true religion in which we completely empty ourselves before God and offer Him our all.
- You and I as God's people need to see people like this widow instead of being so impressed by the big outward shows of religion around us.
- Be impressed with what impressed Jesus.

—*Lesson 12 Discussion*—

1. Are there times you have allowed the pain and injustice inflicted upon you to pull you back from giving your all to Jesus?

2. How can we in a practical way today imitate this poor widow?

3. Do we make excuses to get out of caring for those around us in need?

Lesson 13
Seeing a Woman Who Praised the Lord

Leah—Genesis 29

AND SHE CONCEIVED AGAIN and bore a son, and said, "This time I will praise the LORD." Therefore she called his name Judah. (Genesis 29:35)

What Leah wanted so badly was to be loved by her husband.

Leah comes on to the scene in the book of Genesis as a part of the story of Jacob's life and journeys. Jacob was the grandson of Abraham, the man of faith to whom God promised many things, including: the land of Canaan, a great nation (Israel), and the seed through whom all nations would be blessed. That "Seed" is Jesus Christ the Redeemer of all mankind. Those promises were passed to Abraham's son Isaac, and were in turn given to Jacob, Isaac's son.

It was by trickery and cunning that Jacob took the blessing away from his older twin brother, Esau. Because of this, Esau vowed to kill Jacob. Upon hearing of Esau's promises of murder, Jacob was urged to flee for his life. At the advice of Isaac and Rebekah, Jacob fled east to find Laban, Rebekah's brother. His father instructed him to take a wife from one of Laban's daughters.

When Jacob arrived, who was one of the first people he met? Rachel, Laban's younger daughter. Jacob, as soon as he saw her, went to work for her. He rolled the stone away from the well and watered the sheep. Then he kissed her and wept aloud. Jacob was welcomed into Laban's house and stayed there a month. It was at this point that Laban began negotiations. It was unfair to have Jacob work without pay, so "what shall your wages be?"

Jacob wanted Rachel. But that's not all the Holy Spirit records here.

> Now Laban had two daughters. The name of the older was Leah, and the name of the younger was Rachel. Leah's eyes were weak, but

Rachel was beautiful in form and appearance. Jacob loved Rachel. And he said, "I will serve you seven years for your younger daughter Rachel." Laban said, "It is better that I give her to you than that I should give her to any other man; stay with me." So Jacob served seven years for Rachel, and they seemed to him but a few days because of the love he had for her." (Genesis 29:16–20)

It was all about Rachel. Leah just could not measure up when it came to her sister's physical beauty. Rachel was *va-va-voom,* and Leah was … well just Leah. Jacob loved Rachel. Jacob worked 7 years with his eyes on the prize— Rachel.

But then the 7 years are completed, Jacob has fulfilled his obligation and the wedding is planned. But Laban has a trick up his sleeve. Jacob was a trickster, but certainly met his match in Laban. Laban is going to do the old tactic of bait-and-switch. But we're not talking about selling cars or computers, we're talking about his daughters. Laban is using his own two daughters as pawns, hooks, and tools to manipulate Jacob.

Then Jacob said to Laban, "Give me my wife that I may go in to her, for my time is completed." So Laban gathered together all the people of the place and made a feast. But in the evening he took his daughter Leah and brought her to Jacob, and he went in to her. (Laban gave his female servant Zilpah to his daughter Leah to be her servant.) And in the morning, behold, it was Leah! And Jacob said to Laban, "What is this you have done to me? Did I not serve with you for Rachel? Why then have you deceived me?" Laban said, "It is not so done in our country, to give the younger before the firstborn. Complete the week of this one, and we will give you the other also in return for serving me another seven years." Jacob did so, and completed her week. Then Laban gave him his daughter Rachel to be his wife. (Laban gave his female servant Bilhah to his daughter Rachel to be her servant.) So Jacob went in to Rachel also, and he loved Rachel more than Leah, and served Laban for another seven years. (Genesis 29:21–30)

Imagine being Leah. One could argue that Leah had to agree to this arrangement, and that is possible. However, considering the character of Laban toward Jacob, it is clear that Laban is a manipulator who worked to extend Jacob's contract of employment. Later in Genesis it is revealed that Laban had spent up all his daughter's inheritance and that he changed Jacob's wages 10 times (Genesis 31:7, 14–16, 41). This is a self-serving man. And his daughters are only used for his selfish purposes. Think of what it is like to be Leah in this circumstance.

And in the morning, it was Leah.

People ask, how did Jacob *not* know it was Leah as he was sleeping with her? The simplest answer is that it was dark. Regardless, here is the point: From the first moment she woke up with her husband, Leah was a disappointment. We are not trying to pick on Jacob, we are simply stating facts: And in the morning, it was Leah.

Jacob did so and completed her (Leah's) week. Leah was Jacob's first wife, but she was not his first choice. Jacob was forced to re-enter contract negotiations with his father-in-law. He agreed to give Leah "her week," and then Laban would give him Rachel, too. But Jacob still had to work another seven years. Jacob agreed to the terms because he wanted Rachel. And he dutifully gave Leah "her week." Having relations with Leah was a task to be completed, but Jacob's heart was on another woman. This is Leah's world.

Jacob loved Rachel more than Leah. That's what the Holy Spirit just said. Every day and every glance of Jacob sent Rachel's way painfully reminded Leah that she will never measure up in Jacob's eyes. All she wanted was to be loved. And God saw that Leah was unloved. We'll say more about God and Leah later, but how Leah was being treated garnered the attention of heaven.

> When the Lord saw that Leah was hated, he opened her womb,
> but Rachel was barren. (Genesis 29:31)

The Lord opened the womb of Leah because He saw she was hated (unloved). Leah began to have bouncing baby boy after bouncing baby boy.

Think about it, this was several years of growing and birthing babies. All with one expectation on Leah's part: Surely now Jacob will love her. Leah the baby factory brought these blessings into the world and notice what was on her mind with each of the first three boys. I want my husband Jacob to love me! All of the pain of childbirth, the changes to the body, the waddling around, the discomfort, the stretch marks, the sleepless nights, the nursing, the diapers, etc. would all be worth it if Jacob just loved me.

Baby 1: Reuben

And Leah conceived and bore a son, and she called his name Reuben, for she said, "Because the LORD has looked upon my affliction; for now my husband will love me." (Genesis 29:32)

Look at this! Reuben means "See! A Son!" God has heard me. I'm afflicted. What's her affliction? Not being loved. What did she think with baby one? "For now my husband will love me." See, Jacob, a son! Do you love me now?

Baby 2: Simeon

She conceived again and bore a son, and said, "Because the LORD has heard that I am hated, he has given me this son also." And she called his name Simeon." (Genesis 29:33)

Simeon means "heard." What had God heard? Leah was unloved. Enough time has gone by for two sons to be born, and the situation has not changed, has it?

Baby 3: Levi

Again she conceived and bore a son, and said, "Now this time my husband will be attached to me, because I have borne him three sons." Therefore his name was called Levi. (Genesis 29:34)

Levi's name means "attached." Why did she name him this? Because Leah desperately wanted Jacob to be attached to her as a husband should be.

But had her circumstance changed? No—three babies. Several years. Still unloved.

Please be impressed by the heart of this woman who in the face of such rejection and pain still wanted a loving relationship with her husband. She kept giving herself to him, and she kept birthing children hoping he would change his mind toward her. Think of the wounds she received day after day, month after month, year after year, baby after baby, rejection after rejection, disappointment after disappointment.

Three sons didn't change her relationship with Jacob any more than one did.

Baby Four: Judah

> And she conceived again and bore a son, and said, "This time I will praise the LORD." Therefore she called his name Judah (Genesis 29:35)

Judah means "praise." Why is this so significant and amazing? By the time little baby Judah came, Leah's prayers changed. Her relationship with Jacob had not changed. But she did. She determined: "This time I will praise the Lord."

She did not ask this time for her husband to love her. Not another petition of God for Jacob to see her and be attached to her. Leah's heart this time was settled completely on praising God, no matter what her relationship on earth looked like. Even when what should be hers (love, acceptance, and affection) was not there, she said, "This time, I will praise the Lord."

This process is one of growth. Look at the faith into which God led Leah! It didn't happen right away. Christians get the mistaken idea that these great men and women of faith were always that way from day one. That's not how it works. By the time Judah was born, years had gone by. Leah had learned to praise her Lord no matter what.

"I have learned to kiss the waves that throw me up against the Rock of Ages."
(Charles Spurgeon)

How about you? Are you going to decide to kiss the waves that throw you up against the Rock of Ages? Are you going to choose to believe without wavering that God is perfecting praise from you through pain, rejection, and heartache? Will you in faith determine to trust that God will bring deliverance for others through you? Will you decide to say, 'This time I will praise the Lord!'?

Instead of focusing on what we do not have, cannot have, or may never have, let's turn our eyes to what God has given us. Think about the life of Leah in this light, what did God give Leah? And what did God do through Leah's children?

Leah's story can serve as a symbol of God's salvation and deliverance. The one who was rejected and unloved became the one God lifted up to redeem His people. Moses. Joseph. Jesus. God's people looked at these divinely called deliverers and rejected them. But they were only rejecting God's salvation.

While Jacob was looking at Rachel, Leah's heart was hungering for his love and affection. Her heart was crying out to God. And while Jacob's heart was with Rachel, Leah was building the house of Israel. She was bringing sons into the world that would change history. Leah, the unloved wife, was bringing about through God's divine providence the redemption to Israel.

Think about it, Leah may not have gotten what she requested. She may have never gotten the love of Jacob. We don't know. But what did God give Leah?

God gave Leah at least 7 children (6 sons and 1 daughter). Leah was given Levi, and the priesthood would come through him. The deliverance of Israel from Egyptian oppression was led by Moses and Aaron, descendants of Levi. God gave Leah Judah, and the kingly line in Israel would come through him. David, the descendant of Judah, became King of Israel. David, like Leah, would lead God's people in praise. The Lion of the Tribe of Judah, Jesus Christ, came through Leah. And like Leah, His suffering produced praise (Psalm 22:22–24).

We're all like Leah in some way! God will exalt and work His glory through what men have rejected. Even Jesus was rejected and despised by men (Isaiah 53:3). In Jesus Christ, we are all children of Leah, because we are all Kings and Priests rejected by the world. We, like Leah should proclaim God's praises, even in the midst of suffering (1 Peter 2:9). God sees our beauty and value in Christ, even if no one else does (1 Samuel 16:6–7; 1 Peter 3:1–6).

> Charm is deceitful, and beauty is vain, but a woman who fears the LORD is to be praised. Give her of the fruit of her hands, and let her works praise her in the gates. (Proverbs 31:30–31)

—Lesson 13 Discussion—

1. Are you struggling to praise God as you face great suffering and pain?

2. What have you learned from Leah's faith and determination to praise the Lord?

3. How have you seen in your own life God using the unloved and rejected one to bring about His glory and redemption?

www.ingramcontent.com/pod-product-compliance
Lightning Source LLC
LaVergne TN
LVHW051814080426
835513LV00017B/1944